Taking Initiative on Writing

NCTE Editorial Board

Taking Initiative on Writing

A Guide for Instructional Leaders

Anne Ruggles Gere
University of Michigan

Hannah A. Dickinson
University of Michigan

Melinda J. McBee Orzulak
University of Michigan

Stephanie Moody
University of Michigan

National Council of Teachers of English
1111 W. Kenyon Road, Urbana, Illinois 61801-1096

National Association of Secondary School Principals
1904 Association Drive, Reston, VA 20191-1537

Copy Editor: Theresa Kay
Production Editor: Carol Roehm
Interior Design: Jenny Jensen Greenleaf
Cover Design: Pat Mayer
Cover Image: iStockphoto.com/Ekaterina Romanova

NCTE Stock Number: 49959

A copublication of NCTE and the National Association of Secondary School Principals (NASSP)

Library of Congress Cataloging-in-Publication Data

Taking initiative on writing : a guide for instructional leaders / Anne Ruggles Gere . . . [et al.].
      p. cm.
  Includes bibliographical references.
  ISBN 978-0-8141-4995-9 ((pbk))
  1. English language—Composition and exercises—Study and teaching (Secondary)—United States 2. English teachers—United States. I. Gere, Anne Ruggles, 1944–
  LB1631.T237 2010
  808'.0420712—dc22
                                           2010014119

Contents

Acknowledgments

This book would not have been possible without the time, dedication, and collaborative efforts of many people. Chris Gerben and Tim Green helped to create the Policy Brief, "An Administrator's Guide to Writing Instruction," published in the November 2009 issue of NCTE's *Council Chronicle*, that made us realize the need for this book. Danielle Lillge, Melody Pugh, Christie Toth, and Crystal VanKooten researched and created the online supplemental materials that enhance this project and support the efforts of instructional leaders and teachers of writing. We are grateful to them all. We would also like to thank Greg Hartjes and Genal Hove for their insightful reading and thoughtful feedback at critical points in this process. Finally, we appreciate the support of many people at NCTE: Kurt Austin for seeing this project through from start to finish; Sharon Roth for providing support in conceptualizing the online extensions of this book; Mila Fuller for helping us negotiate with technology; and editor Carol Roehm and copy editor Theresa Kay for their timely and careful attention to the manuscript.

Introduction

The headline reads, "Writing Scores Drop Again," and your phone has been ringing all day with parents, board members, and media representatives asking how you plan to improve writing instruction in your school.

or

A group of business leaders meets with you to talk about how your school can help prepare students for the world of work. They emphasize that they need employees who can write effectively, and they imply that students from your school don't meet their standards.

or

On a return visit, a recent graduate of your school, an excellent student who went on to the university, says that she felt very well prepared in math and science, but she didn't feel ready for college writing.

As an instructional leader, you have probably experienced a scenario like one of these—or it is a situation you are trying to avoid. You no doubt know that writing is increasingly important in the twenty-first century. You may be aware that U.S. workers write more now than at any time in history and that colleges expect students to be able to write well. The responsibility of preparing students to be college- and career-ready writers may be weighing heavily on you, and you might be feeling increasing pressure to take some action. The challenges of high-stakes writing tests; the expectations of stakeholders, including parents, board members, and central administration; and underprepared faculty all contribute to the weight. You've been dealing with local and state writing standards for several years, and now national core standards for writing have emerged. You're likely wondering how to help teachers in your school face the challenges of preparing students for national graduation and workplace standards such as the following:

- Establish and refine a topic or thesis that addresses a specific task and audience.

- Support and illustrate arguments and explanations with relevant details, examples, and evidence.

- Create a logical progression of ideas and events, and convey the relationships among them.

- Develop and maintain a style and tone appropriate to the purpose and audience.

- Demonstrate command of the conventions of standard written English, including grammar, usage, and mechanics.

- Write effectively in a variety of school subjects.

- Assess the quality of one's writing and strengthen it through revision.

- Use technology as a tool to produce, edit, and distribute writing.

English language arts teachers do play key roles in helping students become writers who can meet standards like these, but they cannot do it alone. In fact, some English teachers are not entirely confident about teaching writing. It will take a team effort. You have probably been an instructional leader long enough to know that improving student learning requires effort from many people headed in the same direction. Perhaps you'd like to exert leadership in developing an effective program of writing instruction in your school, but you're not sure where to begin.

This book will help you. It recognizes that you are a busy and cost-conscious instructional leader who needs a way to move forward. It lays out a full sequence of activities designed to assist you in creating an effective program of writing instruction in your school, an effective writing initiative. This sequence includes assessing the current program, developing a plan, implementing action steps, and continuing to sustain and improve the teaching of writing in your school. Each chapter lays out a series of steps to make the process manageable, and each chapter includes the evaluative tools, checklists, and guides that you will need. Each chapter also includes links to online resources developed by the National Council of Teachers of English (NCTE), the association known for its effective professional development for writing teachers. These links are indicated by this icon:

www.ncte.org/books/tiow

However, you may need to address one challenge before turning to practicalities: anticipating the beliefs, myths really, that some people may hold about writing instruction. Some of these myths have a powerful hold in our society because they have some basis in truth, but each one oversimplifies or obscures the real nature of writing and teaching writing. Developing an effective program of writing instruction and explaining it to stakeholders who may know little about teaching writing requires a full understanding of the scope of the task, and that means understanding the myths that may pose obstacles.

Myth: Writing instruction is the responsibility of English teachers alone.

Reality: It's true that English language arts teachers need to provide leadership in writing instruction because they often have greater expertise than their colleagues in other departments. But writing instruction in a school will never be effective if it is not reinforced by teachers in every other department. Furthermore, every content area poses its own challenges and requirements in terms of vocabulary, concepts, topics, and types of writing. Struggling writers have an especially difficult time differentiating between discipline-specific vocabularies, audiences, and genres. The lab report requires a different kind of writing than the research paper on a historical topic, and the features of good writing in both of these content areas need to be taught by science and social studies teachers, respectively, not English teachers.

Myth: Teaching writing means teaching grammar.

Reality: It is true that student writers need to learn how to control the conventions of Edited American English, and there will be occasions where teachers need to offer direct instruction in specific features such as the use of the semicolon or subject-verb agreement. However, attention to issues of grammar falls into what are called Lower-Order Concerns (LOCs) as compared with Higher-Order Concerns (HOCs) in writing instruction. HOCs include such things as learning how to approach and develop a topic, understanding how to address the concerns of a specific audience, organizing ideas so that they are coherent and convincing, and becoming comfortable writing for a variety of purposes. The complexity of learning each of these HOCs demonstrates why writing teachers need to spend most of their time on these rather than grammar and usage.

Myth: Good teachers of writing mark every error every time.

Reality: It is true that teachers need to be alert to errors or infelicities in student writing, but research shows that effective instruction does not mean marking all errors all the time. When teachers read students' early drafts, for example, it is usually more helpful to focus on higher order concerns such as the development of ideas, organization, and overall clarity. Lower-order concerns such as correctness at the sentence level can be addressed more effectively when writers have the general shape of the piece worked out. Similarly, research shows that marking every error every time is less effective than focusing marks on specific issues of usage. Students who receive papers covered with corrections can be so overwhelmed that they don't learn anything from the marks.

Myth: All responsibility for responding to student writing rests with the teacher.

Reality: It is true that teachers have ultimate responsibility for evaluative responses that are tied to grades, and they also have responsibility for giving students regular feedback on writing. This does not mean, however, that teachers are the only ones who can provide helpful responses to writing. Peer response can be effective in helping student writers understand what works well and what needs more development in their writing. For peer response to work most effectively, teachers need to help students learn what constitutes a helpful response to another writer and how to identify both strengths and weaknesses in the writing of others. In addition to peers, members of the community can offer helpful responses to student writing. One of the challenges for most student writers is developing a sense of audience, and responses from others in addition to the teacher helps develop that sense.

Myth: The purpose of school writing is to test students on what they have learned.

Reality: It is true that writing is often used to measure what students have learned in a given subject. The essay exam, the research paper, the report, and the short-answer quiz provide information about what students have learned in a variety of disciplines. But writing can do more than *show* learning; it can also *foster* learning. Through the process of writing, students develop a greater understanding of content in any field. Informal writing such as journal entries and reflections on reading or class discussion can be particularly effective in helping students learn.

In addition to fostering learning, such writing can also lead to improvement in the writing students do to show what they have learned.

Myth: Automatic essay scoring (AES) systems will soon replace human readers of student writing.

Reality: It's true that systems such as ETS's Criterion, Pearson's Intelligent Essay Assessor (IEA), the College Board's ACCUPLACER and WritePlacerPlus, and ACT's Compass are all being used to provide immediate feedback or to evaluate students' writing for placement purposes. However, the feedback such systems provide is limited to a few features of writing, and it is delivered in a highly generic way, roughly equivalent to using a rubber stamp to respond to student writing. Furthermore, these systems are confined to a narrow range of writing types and topics. They may be able to supplement, but they cannot replace the individual attention offered by a teacher who responds to student writing.

Myth: Students should learn everything about writing in elementary school.

Reality: It's true that elementary school students need instruction in writing, and without this background they will have difficulty writing in secondary school. But learning to write is not like learning to ride a bicycle; it's not a set of skills that need no further development once they have been achieved. Learning to write is an ongoing process that extends across all educational levels. Each new subject and each new form of writing poses new challenges; the transition to secondary school, in particular, poses the challenge of writing in many different subjects. The writer who produces imaginative narratives will probably stumble when first asked to write an evidence-based argument. The high school graduate who got As in English will often face unexpected challenges in college writing. Unlike math, where one principle builds on another, learning to write is a spiraling process that requires continuing development and practice throughout the entire experience of schooling.

Myth: Good writing means getting it right the first time.

Reality: It is true that most writers need to do some impromptu composing occasionally, but this method rarely produces the best writing. Good writing results from a more extended process that includes gathering ideas, finding arguments, writing drafts, getting responses to drafts, revising for audience and purpose, and polishing or editing. This process helps writers develop ideas more fully, build connections between points so that the entire piece is clear, and eliminate the errors that can distract readers. Significantly, research shows that students who have extensive experience with using this process for writing do better on timed writing tests than those who have simply practiced timed writing again and again.

Myth: Good writers work alone.

Reality: It's true that writers need some time alone with the keyboard or pen, and we often see images of writers sitting alone at a desk or read real-estate ads with descriptions such as "isolated cottage, suitable for writer." But research shows that writing is a highly social activity. Good writers bounce their ideas off others as they begin a new project; many like to work in busy cafés, offices, or classrooms; they share their drafts with friends and colleagues so that they can revise more effectively; and they often read their work aloud to others to gauge how it will be received. Research on published authors shows—as you can see in the acknowledgments section of any book—correspondence and consultation with friends, family members, and editors. Most writers see themselves as part of a community, sharing ideas, drafts, and questions. It simply isn't true to say that good writers work alone. In fact, a writing initiative can tap into the communal nature of writing and provide wonderful ways to forge relevant connections with families, businesses, and universities.

> **NCTE 0.1** *lists the research that supports the explanations undercutting each of these myths.*
>
> **www.ncte.org/books/tiow**

Understanding, moving beyond, and helping others move beyond these myths to a more complete and research-based account of writing and the teaching of writing will allow you to focus on developing a program of instruction that enables students in your school to become effective writers who are ready for higher education or the workplace. This book can help you accomplish your goals because it lays out each step of the process, showing what needs to be done and including the necessary materials. Each chapter concludes with a implementation scenario based on writing initiatives in real schools.

This is more than a book because every aspect of it is tied to (1) electronic resources that can be downloaded and used immediately; (2) links that connect you to professional development options and other materials focused on writing instruction; and (3) an online forum where you can share ideas with other instructional leaders who are taking initiative with writing. In addition, you can call on the resources of the National Council of Teachers of English, the professional association for English language arts teachers.

Now it is time to turn to the challenging but rewarding project of developing a program of instruction that will prepare your students to write effectively in the twenty-first century. This book is divided into steps that will help you to develop such a program, but, as you know, effective change takes time and continuing attention. Accordingly, the initial steps described in this book are designed to extend over several months, and the later steps over years. Section 1 focuses on the planning process, showing how you can assess your current program of writing instruction, recruit participants in effecting change, and develop goals. Section 2 outlines specific actions, including the development of writing goals and maps, professional development, and additional institutional support. Section 3 provides tools for assessing a wide variety of features including a new program of writing instruction, student learning, teacher quality, and the ongoing implementation of the program. Figure 0.1 shows how the steps outlined in these sections might map onto the school year.

NCTE 0.2 *offers an elaborated version of the following timeline.*

www.ncte.org/books/tiow

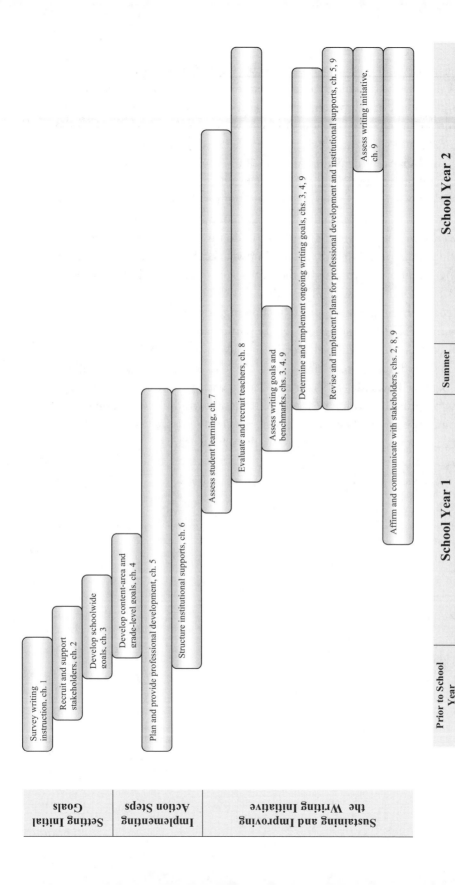

FIGURE 0.1. Sample Timeline for Writing Initiative

1

Setting Initial Goals

This section provides evaluative tools for assessing the state of writing at your school, as well as research-based checklists to guide the creation of schoolwide writing goals.

The chapters in this section will walk you through three key phases of initial goal setting:

Chapter 1: Surveying Writing Instruction in Your School

- Reflect on current writing program.
- Take stock of available writing resources.
- Recruit parents'/guardians' perspectives and support.
- Understand students' writing practices.

Chapter 2: Recruiting and Supporting Stakeholders

- Foster a community of stakeholders.
- Recognize features of effective initiatives.
- Recruit other stakeholders.
- Develop and sustain a leadership team.

Chapter 3: Developing Schoolwide Writing Goals

- Prepare for goal setting.
- Discuss best practices.
- Use collaborative tools to develop short-term and long-term goals.
- Create benchmarks.

Surveying Writing Instruction in Your School

- Survey existing writing practices and attitudes.
- Survey available resources and support.
- Survey students' and parents' perceptions of writing.

Before implementing and maintaining a schoolwide writing program, it is important to consider the current culture of writing instruction in your school. It is likely that teachers within and across content areas have varying attitudes toward writing instruction and assessment. You may also discover that your own beliefs about writing overlap with and diverge from those of teachers. Therefore, it is essential to provide opportunities for teachers and support staff to articulate their perceptions of the current writing curriculum, as well as their objectives for a new writing initiative. This is particularly helpful for schools that are trying to make bridges between school and home communities. In fact, the writing initiative can serve as a key to improving the ways your school engages with the diversity within your community.

It is also important to consider the resources currently available in your school that support student writing. These resources may include the following:

- expertise of teachers, instructional leaders, and support staff
- instructional materials such as curricular guides and textbooks
- technological access to computer labs and software
- professional development resources such as teacher training classes and professional journals

Assessing the availability and quality of these resources will help you make the most of the assets you already have and develop additional opportunities and resources.

Finally, before launching a schoolwide writing initiative, it is important to gather information from both parents/guardians and students about their attitudes toward writing and their perceptions of writing instruction. Asking parents/guardians to participate in the writing initiative conversation will help foster a community of support for students' writing development. Furthermore, because students have diverse writing abilities and instructional needs, and because their curricular and extracurricular writing practices may differ in significant ways, bringing their beliefs, practices, and writing needs into the conversation will assist you in tailoring a writing initiative specific to your students.

This chapter will help you consider how your school's teachers, instructional leaders, and support staff think about the teaching of writing. It will also help you catalog the existing resources and systems of support available in your school. Finally, it will help you consider parents'/guardians' attitudes about writing instruction and students' attitudes toward writing and their extracurricular writing practices. Below you will find four sets of questions, each intended to help you assemble a picture of the writing environment in your school from the perspective of stakeholders. These include the following:

- questions that ask faculty to reflect on the current state of writing instruction;
- questions that ask faculty to assess the current quality and availability of writing resources;
- questions that ask parents/guardians to articulate their beliefs about writing instruction and their role in supporting students' learning; and
- questions that ask students to articulate their beliefs about and uses for writing and writing instruction.

These questions can guide discussions of writing with various stakeholders, and these discussions can help raise awareness of and commitment to the writing initiative. You may also want to collect the views of stakeholders in quantifiable form, and at the NCTE website (www.ncte.org/books/tiow) you can find preconstructed surveys that will yield numerical responses.

Step 1: Reflecting on the Current Writing Program

This step asks administrators and teachers to reflect on the current state of writing instruction and to articulate their beliefs about writing instruction.

If you plan to launch the writing initiative at the beginning of the school year, it will be useful to hold discussions or distribute the questions in survey form several months earlier to allow sufficient time for collection and comparison of responses. As you know, a schoolwide initiative needs a community of stakeholders who are committed to its success. Therefore, if possible, ask *every* teacher, instructional leader, and member of the support staff to weigh in on these questions, either in discussion or in written form on a survey. Especially in the case of larger schools, it might be helpful to appoint departmental leaders who can collect, organize, and synthesize responses. Alternatively, you might ask teachers to meet departmentally or cross-departmentally to discuss the questions and then complete and turn in one set of responses representative of the group's discussion.

NCTE Principles of Writing Instruction

- Everyone has the capacity to write, writing can be taught, and teachers can help students become better writers.
- People learn to write by writing.
- Writing is a process.
- Writing is a tool for thinking.
- Writing grows out of many different purposes.
- Conventions of finished and edited texts are important to readers and therefore to writers.
- Writing and reading are related.
- Writing has a complex relationship to talk.
- Literate practices are embedded in complicated social relationships.
- Composing occurs in different modalities and technologies.
- Assessment of writing involves complex, informed, human judgment.

Once responses to these questions have been compiled, discuss the results. Look for common statements and begin developing a list of agreed-on beliefs. This activity will help the staff analyze the gaps between current practice and future goals. At this point, you may want to compare responses in your school with the principles of good writing instruction identified by NCTE. It may take more than one session to complete this activity, especially if you consider school goals in relation to NCTE Principles of Writing Instruction. However, engaging in this reflective work will assist the staff in developing a writing initiative that is representative of the school community's beliefs, knowledge, and objectives, in addition to being grounded in effective writing instruction.

Question Set 1.1: Reflecting on the Current Writing Program

- Who teaches writing in our school?

- What kinds of writing do students do?

- How do we assess student writing?

- What does assessment tell us about areas of writing where students struggle? Have we done any analysis of external assessment to identify areas where students score low?

- What information do we have about the writing challenges of specific populations such as English language learners or special education students? Is there a gender gap in writing achievement?
- How much writing do students do?
- To what extent is explicit, sustained writing instruction important to students' success in your content area?
- What is the relationship between reading and writing instruction?
- What contributions can instructional leaders, teachers, and parents make to students' writing development?
- How could writing instruction be improved in our school to benefit our students?

NCTE 1.1 *offers this question set in survey format.*

www.ncte.org/books/tiow

Step 2: Taking Stock of Available Writing Resources

This step asks instructional leaders, teachers, and support staff to reflect on the current writing resources available in your school. Because attitudes and dispositions about writing may be closely related to available resources and support networks, it may be useful to ask that teachers respond to question sets 1.1 and 1.2 concurrently. It will also be beneficial for librarians and technology staff to address these questions, as they will have knowledge and expertise about the out-of-classroom writing resources available to faculty and students.

Again, once responses to these questions have been collected, either through conversation or via a survey such as the one available for download, discuss the results. What do the surveys suggest about which resources seem to be most available to the school? Are they being used to their full potential? If not, what changes might be made so that they are? What kinds of resources are missing, insufficient, or ineffective? How might the school invest in, create, or develop writing resources and support in the most cost-effective way?

Question Set 1.2: Taking Stock of Available Writing Resources

- What kinds of support in teaching writing are available for new teachers?

- How and when are relevant books, articles, and other instructional materials shared among teachers and school leaders?

- What kinds of expertise do teachers and support staff already have about the teaching of writing?

- Who could serve as teacher-leaders in writing?

- What kinds of writing-centered professional development opportunities are available for teachers?

- What kinds of technological support are available for students and teachers?

- Besides teachers, who can students ask for help with their writing?

- How can teachers support one another while developing and maintaining the writing initiative?

- In what ways can instructional leaders support writing instruction and improvement?

- What existing programs—a reading initiative, for example—might incorporate or complement a writing initiative?

NCTE 1.2 *offers this question set in survey format.*
www.ncte.org/books/tiow

Step 3: Recruiting Parents'/Guardians' Perspectives and Support

This step asks parents/guardians to articulate their beliefs about the importance of writing instruction in schools as well as their suggestions for improvement. Parents/guardians are crucial stakeholders in any writing initiative. By asking parents/guardians to answer these questions, you are developing the connections between the at-home and at-school network and recruiting parent/guardian support of the writing initiative. In this way, the writing initiative can assist your school with larger goals of connecting to the community. Whether your school is positioned in a district with active support and abundant resources or in one with limited resources and a constant quest for more community involvement, this initiative can provide important links between home and school.

The most effective way to gather parent/guardian responses to these questions is by conducting a survey such as the one available for download. There are several ways to disseminate and collect these surveys. You might decide to post the survey online, mail surveys directly to the parents/guardians, or ask students to take the surveys home and return them to school. If your school has a website or newsletter, you might distribute surveys through these venues. A school open house or parent/guardian night is another important opportunity to distribute surveys; in this setting you can support parents/guardians who might be unfamiliar with school surveys, require a translator, or otherwise require support in completing the survey. The goal is to elicit as many responses as possible, so it might be best to use a combination of distribution methods that will help you reach all families.

Once you have collected the surveys, look for commonalities and suggestions. For example, how might parents/guardians assist in the development and maintenance of the writing initiative? You may find that community members have experience with real-world writing genres, connections to local businesses, or ties to local universities. They may have the time or desire to be involved, concerns about online writing in social networks, or goals to improve their student's preparation for college or the workplace. This survey can help you map out parents'/guardians' concerns, goals, and potential engagement with the initiative.

Question Set 1.3: Recruiting Parents'/Guardians' Perspectives and Support

- How important are strong writing skills to students' success in school? In their futures?
- What school resources do you know about that are available to help students with their writing?
- What kinds of writing should students do in school? Outside of school?
- How might writing instruction be improved in school?
- How can parents/guardians support students in their writing development?

NCTE 1.3 *offers this question set in survey format.*

www.ncte.org/books/tiow

Step 4: Understanding Students' Writing Practices

These questions ask students to reflect on their writing practices both in and out of school. By inviting students to join the writing initiative conversation, you will be better able to tailor instruction, curricula, and resources around their needs and interests. As with the other question sets, responses to these questions should be collected several months prior to launching the new writing initiative. Either through a survey such as the one available for download at the NCTE website (www.ncte.org) or as short-answer questions that teachers compile and synthesize for each class, these questions can be presented as an in-class activity or an assignment to be completed at home. Time permitting, discuss students' responses with them and introduce the writing program initiative.

Attending to Students' Out-of-School Literacy Practices

- Effective teachers value the extracurricular literacy practices and discourse communities in which students participate.
- The writing initiative can help students make bridges between their everyday and academic literacies by supporting students' writing in multiple genres and on a variety of teacher-selected and student-selected topics.

Once the responses have been collected, begin looking for common answers and patterns. How do students' curricular and extracurricular writing practices compare? What do students perceive to be most challenging and most useful about their writing assignments? What aspects of writing would students most like to improve? How do students' perceptions of and goals for writing and writing instruction compare with teachers' and administrators' perceptions and goals? How might the writing initiative help to align these beliefs?

Question Set 1.4: Understanding Students' Writing Practices

- What kinds of writing do you do in school?
- What kinds of writing do you do outside of school?
- What do you find most challenging about school writing assignments?
- What do you find most useful about writing assignments?
- How often do you think writing is explicitly taught (vs. assigned) in school?
- Besides your teachers, who can you ask for assistance with your writing?
- What purposes do writing assignments serve in school?
- When you write outside of school, what purposes do these kinds of writing serve?

- If you could improve one aspect of your writing, what would it be?
- If you could improve one aspect of writing instruction in your school, what would it be?

NCTE 1.4 *offers this question set in survey format.*

www.ncte.org/books/tiow

Implementation Scenario: Surveying to Shape Instruction

Taylor Smith, the principal of Franklin Middle School, introduced survey questions like those in question sets 1.1 and 1.2 to teachers and students. Responses to the surveys produced a lot of information, and Taylor realized that her school could not work on everything at once, so she and her colleagues agreed to focus on something doable that would simultaneously improve students' writing skills and their performance on the writing portion of the state-mandated tests. With this goal in mind, the teachers noted consistent answers around the question about the kind of writing being done in the school. Teachers, students, and staff all agreed that most student writing took the form of short-answer paragraphs in response to questions in textbooks. As one English teacher put it, "I had no idea we were being so consistent in the kinds of assignments we were giving."

In a professional development session, Taylor and the teachers compared the writing they had been assigning with the writing prompt on the state test. The state test asked students to write a narrative, while teachers had been primarily practicing short-answer responses. With this information, the teachers at Franklin decided to begin their writing initiative by expanding the type and length of writing assigned to students, agreeing that this would improve not only students' performances on state tests but also their confidence and versatility as writers.

NCTE 1.5 *offers more examples of instructional leaders implementing principles from this chapter.*

www.ncte.org/books/tiow

Recruiting and Supporting Stakeholders

- Identify and foster a community of stockholders.
- Identify team members across disciplines.
- Promote teacher efficacy, collaboration, and commitment.
- Develop and sustain a leadership team.

After surveying the existing state of writing at your school, it is crucial to find ways to recruit and support stakeholders as you plan the next steps. As a supportive instructional leader, you will want to foster a community of faculty and staff that values writing instruction, assessment, and student achievement. Additionally, you will want to extend this community to include students, their families, and others in the larger school community.

Step 1: Fostering a Community of Stakeholders

Just as with any new initiative, your approach matters. As you already know, you will need to communicate with others that you believe in the many rich possibilities for improving your school with this initiative and share your passion for the new possibilities for supporting students as twenty-first century writers. Your enthusiasm and openness will encourage teachers and other stakeholders to get excited about the possibilities and add their expertise to the pool of resources.

Motivation for most teachers is more than just monetary—most value student learning first and foremost. They're also motivated by opportunities to enhance their teaching or their knowledge base. You will want to involve teachers in a way that helps them see how this initiative connects to their learning, i.e., to their effectiveness in the classroom and their current teaching needs.

Even when teachers are motivated to try new things, change is difficult, and individual teachers will take up the writing initiative at different rates and in varying ways. For instance, consider how teachers have reacted to other initiatives, such as a reading initiative. Will it make sense to pair this writing initiative with current efforts? The Scale of Innovation may help you understand teachers' various responses to the writing initiative.

Scale of Innovation

Innovators: A small percentage of risk-taking teachers who will spend the time to try something new.

Early Adopters: Respected teacher-leaders who will be critical to getting the larger group to take on new techniques.

Early Majority: Teachers who are careful and deliberate, often not willing to commit time or energy to change.

Late Majority: Those who are skeptical about change and often need considerable influence before they change.

Traditionalists: A small group of teachers who will be extremely resistant to change and require significant pressure.

NCTE 2.1 *provides models of response to change.*

www.ncte.org/books/tiow

English Teachers—
Allies or Adversaries?

Your strongest allies might be in the English department, but some of your strongest resistance might come from here as well. The reality is that writing preparation has varied greatly for many English majors and has been virtually nonexistent in many English education programs. This means you may encounter English teachers who want to learn more about writing and/or have remained on the cutting edge of writing instruction. Others, however, may have a deep insecurity that they are not competent writing teachers, and this insecurity may surface as resistance.

As you reflect on what you have learned from discussions and surveys, consider how well you know your faculty/staff.

- Use your knowledge about individual staff members and their strengths, traits, and needs to speculate on how they will respond to the writing initiative.

- Consider how teachers' emotional needs, time constraints, and levels of experience will affect their responses. You want to avoid alienation and encourage buy-in. For instance, who are the superstars in the school who are ready for change? Are these people overcommitted? Are they leaders whom resisters may follow? Who do you anticipate will be the chief complainers or heel-draggers? Do teachers resist out of fear? Lack of time? Insecurity about not looking knowledgeable?

- Head off resistance by encouraging all teachers to share their needs and strengths without fear of being judged. Acknowledge that teachers in disciplines such as math or science may be more likely than English teachers to admit that they don't know what to do with writing in their subject area.

Getting Cross-Departmental Buy-In: How Writing Supports Student Achievement in All Subjects

While a literacy coach and/or English department chair may be strong allies in this process, it is important to avoid making the English department the sole site for this initiative. A schoolwide writing initiative needs the participation of all departments and key players across the school environment; participants need to be convinced that this initiative is about improving learning in their subject. So, how do you explain to a doubtful science teacher or a territorial English teacher that this writing initiative is important for everyone across the school?

You can begin by noting that there is a solid research base supporting your efforts. Research tells us that . . .

- Writing supports learning in all content areas.

- Students who write frequently and across content areas have improved performance on high-stakes tests.

- The public supports writing as a key graduation skill and believes that writing well will help students with standardized tests. Making connections to the larger community and real-world genres can assist the school in making meaningful and culturally responsive connections to students and their families.

- Writing can be used for various steps in learning,

Examples of Cross-Departmental Writing to Learn

Biology teachers have used expressive writing in ways that help students retain more information. Writing assignments such as learning logs, end-of-class summaries, and group writing help students think through problems and engage in hands-on inquiry (from *Because Writing Matters* by Carl Nagin, 2003).

Writing tasks can help students make connections across content areas and subjects. For example, a **language arts teacher** and a social studies teacher might work together and ask students to write a creative piece based on an event or time period currently being studied.

Effective **literacy teachers** discuss the content *and* genres of assigned reading. By drawing students' attention to the structure and conventions of scientific writing, and by asking them to practice writing in these genres, students will better comprehend content material.

such as using writing for exploration, writing to promote inquiry, and writing to generate interpretations.

- Ideas are generated through writing.
- Writing helps students retain information.
- Writing helps students learn the conventions, structures, and formats required in a content area.

Another approach is to use discussion or a survey to identify faculty and staff who are willing to take leadership roles in a writing initiative. In conversations you can explain that a writing initiative includes collecting and analyzing data, developing curriculum, providing professional development, and conducting project evaluation. Asking faculty and staff to answer the following questions will help you identify potential leaders.

Questions to Identify Leaders

- What aspects of a schoolwide writing initiative are of greatest interest to you?
- What level of involvement can you commit to a schoolwide writing initiative?
- What results of the writing initiative are most important to you?
- What professional development will be most important to the success of the writing initiative?

NCTE 2.2 *offers this question set in survey format.*

www.ncte.org/books/tiow

Step 2: Recognize Features of Effective Initiatives

Initiatives that effectively promote teacher learning and engagement start with a groundwork of involvement and validation of teachers and their ideas. Research shows that effective initiatives do the following:

- *Promote teacher efficacy*: Teachers will dedicate more time and effort if they are engaged in the design of activities and with structuring their own professional growth.

- *Encourage teacher collaboration and collegiality*: Teachers who engage in mutually supportive groups take more risks and learn more from/with each other.
- *Validate teacher commitment*: Teachers grow professionally when they are supported by instructional leaders who value their commitment to learning and acknowledge that new learning takes time.

Tips for Promoting Teacher Efficacy

- **Recognize** that there will be multiple ways to proceed and celebrate the creative possibilities and current investments/skills of your teachers.
- **Listen** carefully and communicate the shared vision; be passionate about your vision while also taking a stance as a learner.
- **Consider** the varying levels of teacher experience and proceed accordingly. This may mean providing opportunities for professional development, collaboration, and observing best practices.
- **Construct** a group consensus about schoolwide strengths and needs. Work together to analyze a wide variety of data sources about student writing.
- **Remain** calm in the face of resistance. Sites of resistance usually result from teachers' fear of lack of control or feelings of being overwhelmed. Since teachers will need to work from their own beliefs, now is the time to focus on commonalities and shared goals.

Tips for Encouraging Teacher Collaboration and Collegiality

- **Structure** a team approach. Consider your current school structure and the groups within it. What will be the benefits and challenges if you choose to structure teams by department? In mixed subject area groups? In a voluntary leadership team? By using the current leadership team?
- **Consider** other models. For instance, because elementary teachers teach language arts, science, math, and other subjects, their teams are often structured by grade level rather than subject area. Grade-level teams can help secondary teachers create a cohesive approach to writing across content areas as students move from grade to grade.
- **Choose** a team approach that will foster support and collaboration. Encourage teachers to learn from and with one another.

Tips for Validating Teacher Commitment

- **Support** teachers in their dedication. Be explicit with your acknowledgment of teachers' commitment, not just by providing material resources such as professional development opportunities but also through interpersonal communication.
- **Provide** tangible incentives that help teachers feel supported. Example incentives include providing books for book groups, offering funds for individual professional development, or adding to a professional resource library.
- **Create** supportive spaces. Make sure teams have comfortable and convenient meeting areas, a place for materials, protected meeting time, and funds for resources. See Chapter 6 for more details.

Step 3: Recruit Other Stakeholders

In recruiting stakeholders for this initiative, reach out to the entire faculty and staff. Be sure to include special educators, English language learner instructors, technology advisors, and other key players as you move forward. Depending on your school, other key players may include the PTA, school board, or other community organizations. It is also important not to forget about your students and their families as crucial stakeholders. Try to ensure that stakeholders mirror the racial and ethnic composition of your student body.

NCTE 2.3 *offers a booklist for a professional library on writing instruction.*

www.ncte.org/books/tiow

School Board Members as Stakeholders

As you know, the school board is always interested in student achievement, and often they have to respond to employees who say that high school graduates they hire can't write well enough. Your school board will be interested in the ways this initiative will help student achievement, and you can show how it will benefit the community.

- Explain the multiple ways a writing initiative can support student learn-ing—both in improving short-term motivation and informal writing as well as boosting test scores and other formal measures in the long term. Reading and writing are interconnected, so a writing initiative can pair well with a reading initiative. Attention to writing, since many teachers have little preparation in this area, can add a boost to student success.

- Caution school board members that successful writing initiatives take time and ask them to support your long-term commitment. Consider ways for the school board to participate in and be informed about the writing initiative. School board members might act as authentic audi-ences for writing assignments, for instance.

NCTE 2.4 *offers a PowerPoint presentation that can be adapted for school board and community audiences.*

www.ncte.org/books/tiow

Families as Stakeholders

Successful initiatives pay careful attention to sharing the school's vision with both students and families. The survey process may have helped you connect initially with parents/guardians in the larger community. Here are some ideas for supporting and connecting to these key stakeholders as the writing initiative moves forward:

- Articulate the school's writing philosophy to parents/guardians. You could write to them in letter form or in an e-newsletter. You can also provide updates about the writing initiative. Talking to them about the writing plan and explaining key ideas will help them understand what is going on and support their children.

- If you serve a population of students whose parents struggle with writing themselves, it may be helpful to partner with a community group such as Head Start or another adult education program and make writing a community focus.

- Some school communities have students whose parents write regularly for work. Tap into these resources, but remember: people have very strong—and sometimes old-fashioned—beliefs about how writing should be taught. You'll have to work to communicate why your school's approach best serves their children.

- Provide ways for them to support the school's writing initiative. Other schools have used parent/guardian writing workshops, book clubs, and study groups. You can offer a specific informational night or nights dedicated to teaching parents/guardians about the kinds of writing strategies students are learning in their classes, or you can offer parent/guardian education sessions during family conferences.

Key Writing Terms to Explain to Parents/Guardians

Revision/editing: When *revising*, students are rethinking or conceptualizing in writing; *editing* means working on spelling, punctuation, or sentence structure.

Content-area writing: Successful high school and college writers know how to write differently across school subjects, including writing for audiences other than their teachers.

Informal/formal writing: A range of writing assignments in different genres will help student writers. Informal writing includes low-stakes and impromptu writing; formal writing is often composed over time and graded.

Higher-Order Concerns/Lower-Order Concerns: HOCs, as they are often called, refer to the conceptual dimensions of writing such as ideas, organization, and originality, whereas LOCs refer to surface features such as spelling, punctuation, and usage.

New media writing: Being technology-savvy is important for twenty-first century writers. Students need opportunities to practice using new technology as part of the writing process.

NCTE 2.5 *offers more terms and detailed definitions that may be useful for explaining the writing initiative to parents/guardians.*

www.ncte.org/books/tiow

Students as Stakeholders

In the end, the students are your main stakeholders. The whole point of this initiative is to focus on your students as writers and learners in the twenty-first century. You will want to communicate this to them and explain that there may be changes necessary to supporting them as learners. However, you also want to acknowledge what is already working and communicate your goals to build on this.

You may even include students on some of the planning committees. Any changes brought on by this initiative should be based on shared goals as a school community, and students will be more connected and motivated if they feel they are a genuine part of the community.

Step 4: Develop and Sustain a Leadership Team to Help You Build a Writing Program

Developing and sustaining some kind of leadership team can help you manage the tasks ahead and should be a first step as you move toward establishing schoolwide goals. Members of an effective leadership team will need time as you invite them to lead the school in assessing current strengths and professional development needs. Team members will need to develop an understanding of the school community and review / investigate what they don't know.

Options for Structuring Your Team

Existing School-Based Leadership Team
Some schools already have school-based leadership teams that include department leaders from across the school. These team members may need support and training in how to take up a writing initiative. They may also benefit from attending a summer institute or a professional development sequence about writing. Be wary of this initiative becoming sidelined on an already full leadership team agenda.

New Writing Initiative Team
One benefit of recruiting teacher-leaders for a new leadership team is that you can form a team that will focus on writing specifically. Members can focus on gathering specific information on writing across the school community. If your school already has a reading initiative or School Improvement team, they might also work in conjunction with these leaders. Results of question set 2.2 can help you identify team members.

Literacy Coach

If your school has a literacy coach, you will want to consider the coach's current role and how to incorporate this role into your leadership structure. However, be sure not to dump this project onto an already overworked coach who is more focused on reading. It will work better to tap into new and existing leaders who feel passionately about the writing initiative.

As your team begins and continues its work, it will be important to remember that teachers involved in any initiative may proceed through a series of steps, as Figure 2.1 shows.

NCTE 2.6 *offers more material on school and faculty change.*

www.ncte.org/books/tiow

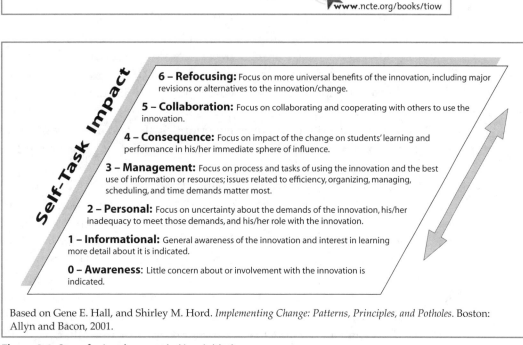

Based on Gene E. Hall, and Shirley M. Hord. *Implementing Change: Patterns, Principles, and Potholes.* Boston: Allyn and Bacon, 2001.

Figure 2.1. Steps for Involvement in New Initiatives

Implementation Scenario: Recruiting a Leadership Team

Trevor Abernathy was a new principal at Forest High School. The students at Forest had scored at the bottom of the state-mandated writing test for several years and morale throughout the school was extremely low. Teachers at Forest had been working without a contract for two years, and they had no enthusiasm for any new initiative. Trevor knew he had to think creatively about how to recruit and support faculty and staff to become stakeholders in a writing initiative. He suspected teachers wouldn't respond to a survey, but keeping in mind questions like those in question set 2.2, he began looking for writing initiative leaders. Rather than demand that teachers participate, Trevor tried to capitalize on the teachers' and school's strengths.

For example, Forest had been successful at getting grants to support initiatives, especially in technology. As a result, the school had several well-supplied computer labs, but they were underutilized due to staffing issues. Latisha Brown, a member of the English department, had previously worked in a writing lab at a nearby college. By rearranging teaching schedules, Trevor was able to give Latisha a part-time assignment to develop a writing lab for the school, something she had wanted to do, and this was enough to persuade her to take a leadership role in the writing initiative.

Forest High School also had an ROTC program, and Roger Dykstra, one of its instructors, a social studies teacher, had expressed concerns about the writing abilities of the ROTC recruits. In conversations with Trevor, Roger also expressed concerns about the space allocated to the ROTC program, particularly the storage facilities for uniforms and equipment. In a meeting about how to best support students in the ROTC program, Trevor and Roger agreed to make space allocation and writing improvement priorities. To do so, Trevor reassigned space to accommodate the ROTC uniforms and equipment and Roger agreed to join the leadership team for the writing initiative.

Trevor knew that for the writing initiative to get off the ground, he would need support from parents, teachers, and staff. Martha Broad, a teacher's aide who had been moved to the library when the professional librarian's position was cut, was the obvious choice. She knew the families of many of the students, and she cared deeply about them. Students knew that they could talk to Martha if they had a problem, she kept energy bars and other snacks in her desk drawer for the kids who came to school hungry, and she often advocated for students in disciplinary cases. Trevor quietly began contributing to Martha's snack supply and talked to her about the students' academic needs. He learned that they both shared a concern about the students' writing skills. Martha hesitated to join the leadership team, but Trevor convinced her that he was serious about helping the students at Forest. With Martha, Latisha, and Roger, Trevor had a leadership team that could help him begin a writing initiative.

NCTE 2.7 *offers more examples of instructional leaders implementing principles from this chapter.*

www.ncte.org/books/tiow

Developing Schoolwide Writing Goals

- Discuss best practices.
- Collaboratively create long-term writing goals.
- Create benchmarks.

With stakeholders on board, it is tempting to start work immediately and make changes to the curriculum, schedule, and budget. However, successful writing initiatives are not built by one person and they don't happen immediately. This chapter contains resources to help you think about ways to collaboratively create long-term schoolwide writing goals with appropriate benchmarks.

Step 1: Prepare for Goal Setting

Your faculty and staff are your school's best resources for determining what sorts of writing goals are necessary and attainable, and they will have many creative strategies for attaining these goals. Your role in this process includes four key actions.

Build in adequate time to set goals as a school community.

Set aside a professional development day, several faculty meetings, or some summer planning time to create your schoolwide writing goals. Goal-setting conversations are inspirational, but sometimes they also feel frustrating; without adequate time to move past frustrations and arrive at consensus, it will be difficult to achieve buy-in across the school. Depending on the size of your school, you may work in smaller groups or have staggered meetings, but it is essential to find a way for all faculty and staff to participate in this process. Step 3 of this chapter offers models for goal setting.

Prepare to guide faculty and staff to a consensus on essential writing goals.

Meet with your writing leadership team to determine how you will structure the goal-setting sessions with faculty and staff. The rest of this chapter provides suggestions for structuring these sessions that you and your writing leadership team can consider. Encourage your leadership team to facilitate these activities, but feel free to make suggestions if an important goal such as "use the writing process in every classroom" is missing.

Be creative but realistic about the resources your school has to meet writing goals.

In these goal-setting sessions, you'll hear faculty/staff say things such as "we don't have enough time in the schedule to teach writing" or "how can I focus on new media writing skills when we don't have enough computers for my class?" Examine your budget, the school schedule, and school resource allocations to be prepared to answer these sorts of questions.

Examine school goals in relation to the Common Core Standards initiative.

An alliance of the National Governors Association and the Conference of Chief State School Officers has produced standards for national use. These standards represent a floor, not a ceiling, for student writing achievement. Many schools will aim for higher standards than the Core Standards for writing, but these standards do offer a place to begin, a way to think about student achievement. And, as Chapter 4 shows, it is also important to consider how standards can be translated into grade-level benchmarks for student achievement in writing.

Tips for Building Writing Resources

- **Make contact with local organizations:** Many areas have writers-in-schools programs, a National Writing Project site, or university writing outreach programs that will work with your faculty, staff, and students for free. .
- **Reach out to volunteer writing coaches:** Retired professionals, college students, and parents all have writing expertise to offer ranging from business writing, to college admissions essays, to new media writing.
- **Research technology grants:** New hardware and software may be necessary to support new media writing skills. Try to find grants that include funding for professional development and technology support staff.
- **Think creatively about school space:** Could the computer lab be reconfigured as a writing center? Would replacing desks with tables help facilitate writing workshops and collaborative writing?
- **Embed writing into all school initiatives:** Your school may have other initiatives, ranging from reading development to service projects in the community, and the writing initiative will be most effective if writing is integrated into each of them. Additionally, you may be able to use the resources or structures allocated for an existing initiative. For instance, resources from a technology initiative could be aligned to your writing goals. Or, if you're also introducing an initiative to improve state test scores, find test-prep resources that use writing as a primary learning tool.
- **Be flexible but realistic about scheduling and staffing needs:** Could you create longer literacy blocks? Could the literacy coach push into the science classes? Could the social studies and ELA teachers team-teach a unit on research and writing? Can you create smaller writing classes for struggling students?

NCTE 3.1 *offers a full list of Common Core Standards and Benchmarks in Writing for grades 6–12.*

www.ncte.org/books/tiow

Step 2: Discuss Best Practices

As you know, technological advances, changing workplace demands, and cultural shifts are making writing more important than ever. Two-thirds of America's salaried employees have some writing responsibility, and employers report that writing skills affect hiring and promotion decisions. Writing skills may also predict students' academic success in college. Yet current studies indicate that many students write little and infrequently, even in their English classes. The growing demand for good writers requires secondary schools to play their part in preparing all students for a changing world. By incorporating best practices of writing instruction into your school's curriculum and mission, you will increase students' academic and job successes, create opportunities for civic participation, and enhance critical thinking skills necessary in today's

Best Practices in Writing Instruction
- Present writing as a process.
- Make transparent reading and writing connections.
- Promote writing to learn.
- Assign writing in multiple, real-world genres.
- Encourage writing across the content areas.
- Teach grammar in context.
- Provide authentic writing assessment.
- Value extracurricular writing practices.
- Invest in new media writing instruction.
- Encourage writing as a social practice.

world. Incorporating best practices in the teaching of writing will also improve your standardized test scores. As students learn to brainstorm, write, revise, and edit, they are building foundations that will help them on standardized assessments, in college, and at work. If you are in a school with achievement gaps, these best practices will be particularly important to meeting your goals for equitable student achievement. Writing instruction is an excellent way to help all students become more aware of and comfortable with privileged real-world and academic writing and reading.

By examining the survey data you've collected in relation to best practices in writing instruction, you can provide your faculty and staff with important tools for creating appropriate and meaningful goals. A discussion of this information will also help faculty/staff develop a common vocabulary for talking about the teaching of writing. Work with your writing leadership team to determine how best to present this material to the faculty/staff.

Presenting Best Practices

Consider creating a forum for presenting information about best practices in writing instruction. If you instituted study groups in the stakeholder stage or if the writing leadership team has learned about best practices in writing instruction, ask these groups to present their findings. Alternatively, you could have faculty examine the document titled "NCTE's Beliefs about the Teaching of Writing."

NCTE 3.2 *offers a copy of "NCTE's Beliefs about the Teaching of Writing" and other resources or best practices.*

www.ncte.org/books/tiow

Activities to Maximize Teacher Engagement with Best Practices

- **Jigsaw**: A team of knowledgeable teachers presents a different writing practice to a number of small groups. Then departments come together to share what they learned.

- **Mini-study groups**: Before the staff meeting, have staff/faculty read a description of an effective writing teacher or school. The whole staff can read the same piece, or different pieces can be assigned to small groups.

- **Policy briefs**: Present an NCTE policy brief (a summary of relevant research) to the staff. In departments or grade-level groups, have staff discuss how the research applies to their instructional practices.

As you know, it is important to present best practices in a concrete fashion without overly simplifying complex material. It may take teachers time to adjust to new approaches in writing instruction; in this phase, it is useful to present this information as a resource rather than an ultimatum. Teachers may also respond well to hearing how other teachers or other schools have put these best practices into place. New pedagogical approaches benefit from models, and it will also be important for your faculty/staff to see that these best practices really do work.

Examining Survey Data

Before meeting with the whole school, the writing leadership team should have worked through the results of the survey data to present them in a comprehensive fashion. They might point out common themes, describe students' experiences with writing instruction and their writing goals, and discuss trends and differences in teachers' beliefs about writing. After these data have been presented, teachers might compare the emerging portrait of writing instruction with that of "NCTE's Beliefs about the Teaching of Writing" and discuss their reactions in small groups. These groups could be organized around grade level, department, or heterogeneously. You could ask them to respond to questions such as, What surprised them? What schoolwide strengths emerge? What are some areas for improvement? Come back together and share these impressions as a group.

Step 3: Collaboratively Create Long-Term Writing Goals

Meaningful goals are created from the bottom up, using the knowledge and experiences of your faculty / staff. Goal-setting conversations are also helpful for bringing conflicting approaches or priorities to the surface.

Brainstorming

At this stage, it is important to provide a space for all departments, teachers, and staff members to share a wide range of writing goals. Some ideas will be long term, some will be short-term benchmarks, and others will target institutional needs; some goals, such as implementing authentic schoolwide writing assessments, will align with contemporary research on writing and others, such as implementing daily timed-writing tasks, will not. No matter what the scope or significance of each brainstormed goal, it's important to record it—value free—so all stakeholders feel heard. Depending on the size and disposition of your faculty / staff, you might choose to brainstorm as a whole staff, writing each response on a whiteboard or using an LCD projector. You might choose to brainstorm in small groups before the big group meeting or simply brainstorm in small groups and have the writing leadership team consolidate the responses before sharing them with the whole group.

What Makes a Good Writing Goal?

*Building a sustainable writing program takes time. Most schools plan on committing **at least two years** of focused attention to a writing initiative. Or your school can spread the steps over a longer period if this makes sense in conjunction with current initiatives.*

Long-term writing goals are

- *Created collaboratively*
- *School-specific*
- *Ambitious*
- *Attainable*
- *Measurable*

Clustering

As a staff / faculty, begin clustering all the goals you have created (see Figure 3.1). Again, this can be done as a whole group or in smaller groups, but it is important that the whole faculty / staff is a part of this process, so that all stakeholders can see their goals taken into account. As you cluster, you'll want to discuss why certain goals ought to be categorized together, with an eye to ultimately creating two-year goals that are ambitious, measurable, and attainable. You'll also want to discuss writing goals that seem contradictory. For example, have a conversation about

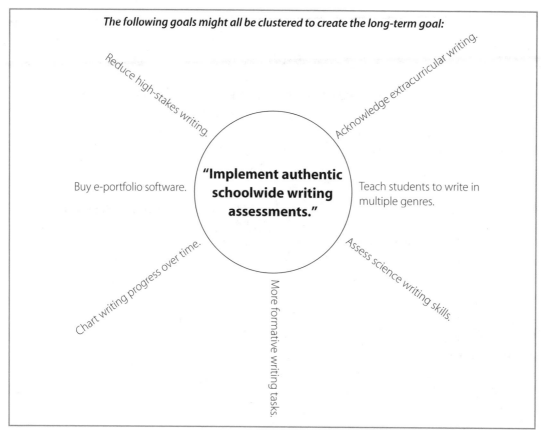

The following goals might all be clustered to create the long-term goal:

Reduce high-stakes writing.

Acknowledge extracurricular writing.

Buy e-portfolio software.

"Implement authentic schoolwide writing assessments."

Teach students to write in multiple genres.

Chart writing progress over time.

Assess science writing skills.

More formative writing tasks.

Figure 3.1. Clustering of Goals

whether more in-class, timed writing will really meet the larger goal of implementing authentic schoolwide writing assessment. This will help identify discrepancies among the faculty in writing values and philosophies and provide a forum for working out some of these discrepancies. Issues that remain unresolved can always be further researched and returned to later.

Prioritize Writing Goals

Ask faculty/staff to begin prioritizing long-term writing goals. You might do this by having individuals, grade-level teams, or departments rank their top three goals. Gather these rankings and present them to the faculty. As a group, discuss how these goals might work together. Discuss whether any major areas seem missing: Is assessment included? How about content-area writing? Does every department have a stake in these goals? Finally, discuss how these goals will work in conjunction with state standards, standardized testing, and other school initiatives. Finalize a list of three to five long-term writing goals.

Acknowledge the Role of State and National Testing

Your faculty, staff, and other stakeholders may be concerned about whether these new writing goals will actually help students on their standardized tests. These concerns should be taken seriously because test scores can affect the lives of students, teachers, and the school itself.

However, you can remind teachers that writing initiatives that follow best practices in writing instruction have been shown to improve high-stakes test scores. Take some time with your faculty/staff to examine each writing goal. Ask them to consider how meeting this goal will align with state standards and affect student performance on standardized tests. In all likelihood, the goals your faculty/staff write will align with state standards and high-stakes test expectations; in fact, they will probably be more ambitious! However, be prepared for tweaking some goals or adding a new one to ensure that your goals will also help students meet state and national expectations.

Step 4: Create Benchmarks

Creating and monitoring short-term benchmarks will help to ensure that the school is making progress toward its long-term writing goals. A combination of institutional and schoolwide benchmarks will ensure that faculty/staff are supported and accountable throughout this writing initiative.

Institutional Benchmarks

Writing achievement will improve with smaller class sizes, increased class time devoted to writing instruction, professional development, and new technologies. If you can make even small moves toward some of these changes, you will communicate to stakeholders that this writing initiative is being taken seriously. As a group, list the resources and institutional supports that will be required to meet each long-term goal. To implement authentic schoolwide writing assessments, will you require e-portfolio software, professional development, storage space, or a steering committee? After you have generated a list of resources and institutional supports, begin to brainstorm some creative solutions. Can you apply for a technology grant? Work with a local university? Transform a supply closet into a portfolio storage area? You may not be able to provide all of the resources and institutional supports that your faculty/staff request, but by brainstorming together, you will communicate that you're committed to making change, and they will be able to contribute to the prioritizing of school resources. At the same time, be realistic and straightforward about which changes are simply not possible.

Instructional Benchmarks

It is important to build in short-term benchmarks to ensure that you're on track to meeting your long-term writing goals. Unlike the departmental benchmarks that faculty/staff will create in content-area teams, these benchmarks should apply to the whole school. For example, if your schoolwide goal is to increase the quantity of student writing—in and out of school—by 80 percent, your first benchmark may be to increase the quantity of student writing by 5 percent. Benchmarks are meaningless if they cannot—or won't—be monitored. Make sure that your benchmarks are measurable and be realistic about how often they can be measured. Your faculty/staff will do a great job of thinking creatively about these sorts of issues. For example, they might choose to post a chart in each homeroom on which students write down the number of pages they write each week. Or they might create a database into which each teacher enters the number of pages they have required students to write that week. Systems like these would make this writing goal simple to measure regularly; however, it is crucial that faculty/staff generate these benchmarks and measurement strategies, rather than feeling as if they have been mandated. Talk to your faculty/staff about what support you can provide in measuring each benchmark.

To facilitate benchmark brainstorming, consider breaking your faculty/staff into small groups and assigning each group a different goal; each group should create benchmarks for the goal they have been assigned. Come back together and assess as a group whether the benchmarks are attainable, measurable, and appropriate to the long-term goal. At this stage, it is especially important that instructional leaders are realistic about the role they can play in supporting the achievement and measurement of these instructional benchmarks.

Table 3.1 is just one example of how your school community might set up schoolwide benchmarks. In this version, the school has decided to focus intensively for 50 weeks on the writing goal: "Implement authentic schoolwide

Table 3.1. Sample Institutional and Instructional Benchmarks for Meeting the Writing Goal: *Implement Authentic Schoolwide Writing Assessments*

Weeks 1–4	Weeks 5–8
Instructional Leader: Introduce initiative to staff; create a steering committee. **Teachers/Staff**: In department groups, identify one authentic assessment that will serve as Writing Sample 1.	**IL**: Research and report on e-portfolio grants, or research a schoolwide, paper portfolio system. **Teachers/Staff**: Collect first draft of Writing Sample 1 from each student in each class.
Weeks 9–12	**Weeks 13–16**
IL: Apply for e-portfolio grant, or organize a paper portfolio collection system. **Teachers/Staff**: Assign and collect a revision of Writing Sample 1 from each student in each class.	**IL**: Plan a professional development session on evaluating writing samples. **Teachers/Staff**: Evaluate Writing Sample 1, record each student's strengths and weaknesses, and identify struggling students.
Weeks 17–20	**Weeks 21–24**
IL: Design and implement support (such as cross-class tutoring or community volunteers) for struggling students. **Teachers/Staff**: Identify a second authentic assessment that will serve as Writing Sample 2.	**IL**: Install e-portfolio software. **Teachers/Staff**: Collect first draft of Writing Sample 2.
Weeks 25–28	**Weeks 29–32**
IL: Plan and lead a professional development session on e-portfolios or paper portfolios. **Teachers/Staff**: Assign and collect a revision of Writing Sample 2 from each student in each class.	**IL**: Begin development of schoolwide reports on authentic writing assessment. **Teachers/Staff**: Evaluate Writing Sample 2 and record each student's progress.
Weeks 33–36	**Weeks 37–40**
IL: Introduce students to e-portfolio/paper portfolio system and upload or collect Writing Samples 1 and 2 from each class; complete schoolwide reports. **Teachers/Staff**: Evaluate individual student e-portfolios/paper portfolios and record progress in each content area.	**IL**: Meet with parents to discuss e-portfolios/paper portfolios and schoolwide reports. **Teachers/Staff**: Complete evaluation of individual student e-portfolios/paper portfolios and record progress in each content area.

Weeks 41–50

Instructional Leader:
- Plan for cycle 2 of authentic writing assessment: schedule outside consultants, set aside professional development time, create budget priorities.
- Fund and facilitate training for department heads and teachers in assessing student writing.
- Meet with the superintendent to present progress and discuss districtwide institution of authentic writing assessment.

assessments." However, at your school you may decide to focus on three goals over a 150-week period. Especially important to note, however, is that instructional leaders, teachers, and staff all have important roles to play in meeting each benchmark.

Implementation Scenario: Data-Driven Goal Setting

Data from a high school in New Jersey showed a significant achievement gap along race and class lines even though the good writing scores of a majority of the students masked the problem. Initially, Rebecca Rubin, the language arts coordinator, thought in terms of a program targeting the struggling students, but several teachers persuaded her that it would be better to develop a writing initiative that would benefit all students.

With the help of interested teachers and staff, who formed the leadership team for the writing initiative, Rebecca sought administrative support, conducted surveys, and looked at assessment data to begin the process of setting goals for the writing initiative. It quickly became clear that a successful writing initiative needed teachers in every subject, not just English teachers, so Rebecca solicited help from coordinators in other fields. Together they identified and recruited a core group of teachers to participate in a professional development program offered by the local site of the National Writing Project. This program gave teachers multiple strategies for incorporating writing into every subject area.

Rebecca and her team decided to focus initially on just one level, the sophomore year. Teachers in all subjects taken by sophomores met to decide on their goals for student writing. Initially, they had several goals, including fluency in writing, use of evidence in writing, incorporation of subject-specific vocabulary in writing, and use of appropriate conventions in writing. Eventually, the team decided to limit its goals to two: fluency and use of evidence. They argued that these were goals that would best serve struggling writers as well as the general population. Convinced by research showing that writing fosters learning in any subject, teachers agreed to aim for the goal of regular writing, both informal and formal, in all classes, assuming that this would be the best way to give all students an opportunity to develop fluency or ease in producing writing on a regular basis. Use of evidence was the other goal, and teachers agreed that it, too, should be a goal for teachers in every discipline.

NCTE 3.3 *offers more examples of instructional leaders implementing principles from this chapter.*

www.ncte.org/books/tiow

2

Implementing Action Steps

This section describes concrete steps instructional leaders can take to help teachers develop and implement discipline-based writing goals.

The chapters in this section explain three areas that will help you implement the goals of your school's writing initiative.

Chapter 4: Develop Content-Area and Grade-Level Writing Goals

- Support writing in content areas.
- Support grade-level and departmental teams.
- Create grade-level and departmental writing goals.

Chapter 5: Providing Professional Development

- Base professional development on research and best practices.
- Create timely and cost-conscious professional development.

Chapter 6: Structuring Institutional Support

- Address class size.
- Consider teacher assignments.
- Evaluate technology.
- Reconsider key factors in writing initiative.
- Plan to meet the needs of diverse learners.

Developing Content-Area and Grade-Level Writing Goals

- Support writing in the content areas.
- Support teams.
- Create departmental writing goals.

An effective writing initiative is not limited to the English department but extends across all subjects. Each content area has content-specific knowledge, and students need to learn how to express this knowledge in their writing. Indeed, the Common Core Standards in science and history emphasize the importance of maintaining writing standards similar to those in English language arts. While it may seem prudent to teach students writing "basics" in their English classes before requiring them to engage in writing across the disciplines, all students—especially struggling writers—benefit from being actively encouraged to see the forms writing takes in different disciplines. Having to discuss and write about the difference between, say, a lab report and an essay about the Civil War can help students to transfer knowledge into various disciplines. This can help improve students' academic writing skills, but it will also improve reading comprehension; your initiative's focus on writing is a great way to help students at all levels find academic success. Creating clear writing goals for each content area will help make this process more transparent to teachers and students. This chapter provides materials to help teachers of each subject develop writing goals and benchmarks that will enhance content-area learning in addition to supporting the schoolwide writing initiative.

Step 1: Support Writing in the Content Areas

As you know from developing schoolwide goals, goal setting is difficult if faculty/staff don't have a common vocabulary, some shared values, and a gen-

Important Definitions in Content-Area Writing

Writing across the curriculum (WAC) assumes that writing can both foster and demonstrate learning in a variety of subjects or disciplines. The goal of a WAC program is to prepare students for a variety of disciplinary reading and writing contexts.

Writing in the disciplines (WID) has much in common with WAC, but the emphasis is different. It focuses on specific genres, vocabulary, and other conventions of a given discipline.

Writing to demonstrate knowledge gives students opportunities to demonstrate what they have learned in a given unit of study. Even this sort of writing benefits from a process approach.

Writing to learn can help students understand, process, and think critically about course material. These activities are often informal and help students build knowledge, rather than have it tested.

Functional grammar is an approach to grammar that sees language not as a set of rules, but as a set of choices. This encourages students to adopt syntaxes, genres, and language appropriate to each disciplinary context, ultimately making them more metacognitive and versatile writers and readers.

Genre can be a useful term for talking about different types of writing in content areas. Lab reports, memos, mathematical proofs, and webpages all have their own linguistic, stylistic, and social rules that students will benefit from learning.

eral sense of the school's strengths and weaknesses in writing instruction. Some content-area teams may be familiar with key concepts in content-area writing, but others may have limited experience with teaching writing in their content area. Faculty and staff will need support as they become familiar with the best practices of content-area writing instruction, and it's crucial that this groundwork is laid before content-area and grade-level teams move on to setting goals. Analyzing student writing samples within departments is also a useful way to help teams develop common goals and vocabularies.

> **NCTE 4.1** *offers resources on content-area writing.*
>
> www.ncte.org/books/tiow

Why Does Content-Area Writing Instruction Matter?

Content-area writing instruction serves multiple purposes. Such instruction will be useful to students as they enter careers with specific writing and genre expectations; it will help students develop the critical awareness and versatility necessary to write in twenty-first century contexts and genres; it will help students determine the appropriate language and genre for a given writing context, including high-stakes tests; and writing helps students to comprehend, analyze, and remember discipline-specific concepts.

- Imagine that a student, Andre, has written primarily literary analysis in school. He can break down the rhyme and meter of a Langston Hughes poem with ease, but can he write a grant proposal for the children's poetry workshop he hopes to begin?

  Some teachers will dismiss this example, claiming that the writing skills Andre developed in his English class should transfer to his grant writing. They're right. These skills should transfer, but only if Andre has been taught to identify the language and conventions of a wide range of written genres, including mathematical, persuasive, and business genres, all of which he'll need to use in his grant proposal. That's what content-area writing instruction does—it helps students see that writing doesn't happen only in English class and teaches them to transfer writing skills across contexts.

- Imagine that another student, Rosa, is struggling to understand states of matter in her science class. She has read and reread the textbook, created diagrams, and done experiments, but she is still struggling with the scientific concept. Finally, Rosa's teacher asks her to create a story explaining how water turns from a solid, to a liquid, to a gas. An imaginative student, Rosa turns a water molecule into a superhero and describes her adventures through the states of matter. By putting this scientific process into a coherent story, Rosa's comprehension and recall improve.

Some teachers will say that they've been giving assignments like this for years, but it doesn't mean that they know how to teach writing. Explain that they're wrong—they are writing teachers! While some writing assignments are used to assess students' writing skills, writing in the content areas should also be used to help students learn disciplinary concepts. This way, students come to see that writing can be a low-stakes and important tool for learning.

Best Practices in Content-Area Writing Instruction

Support your faculty/staff as they explore four components of content-area writing instruction that have been shown to improve student writing achievement: using writing to learn; emphasizing writing as process; connecting writing to reading; and writing in multiple, academic, and real-world genres (see Table 4.1). These best practices are easily aligned with content-area goals. For example, if the science department would like students to practice using scientific vocabulary, they could emphasize the reading-writing connection; this connection helps students identify the strategies science writers use when incorporating technical science vocabulary, thus enhancing students' ability to employ those strategies in their own science writing.

The chart in Table 4.1 should not replace meaningful professional development that emphasizes best practices in content-area writing. Instead, it is meant to begin facilitating discussion around content-area writing goals. You will probably have some content-area teachers who have never thought of themselves as teachers of writing. You—along with your leadership team—can use these four

Table 4.1. Best Practices in Content-Area Writing Instruction

Writing to Learn	Examples
Writing to learn can help students understand, process, and think critically about course material. Therefore, it is an important tool to help students learn content-specific material, to evaluate their own understanding of that topic, and/or to develop expertise about it. Teachers who create writing assignments that begin by engaging students in informal writing-to-learn activities set the stage for students to demonstrate—in final, polished writing—a fuller understanding of the topic at hand.	**Science:** Write a journal entry describing photosynthesis in your own words. **Math:** Write a step-by-step description of how you solved for $3x + 2y = 3$ and $x = 3y - 10$. **Social Studies:** Create a T-chart comparing the goals of the Bread and Roses strike of 1912 to those of a contemporary labor movement. **Language Arts:** Write a paragraph predicting what you think will happen next in *Invisible Man*. **Physical Education:** Create a diagram—with descriptive captions—identifying the muscle group involved in throwing a Frisbee, kicking a soccer ball, and jumping rope.
Writing in Multiple, Academic, and Real-World Genres	**Examples**
The twenty-first century demands that effective writers possess a wide range of writing skills and varying approaches to writing tasks. Writers need to understand and respond to many different rhetorical situations, addressing multiple audiences for a variety of purposes. Therefore, encourage departments to be creative when assigning writing tasks. Providing students with access to the conventions of privileged genres and opportunities to write in them will not only expose students to the requirements of various content-specific genres, but will also enhance student engagement with course content.	**Science:** Write an op-ed outlining steps young people can take to combat global warming. **Math:** Prepare a presentation in which you present your analyses of polling data from the presidential primaries. **Social Studies:** Write a book review of the nonfiction book you selected about the women's rights movement. **Language Arts:** Write a poem—in the spirit of Anzaldúa—that describes the borderlands you've experienced. **Business:** Write a proposal and budget plan for a new school store.
The Reading-Writing Connection	**Examples**
Reading and writing skills are closely connected. For students to become competent readers in multiple genres, it is essential that they are familiar with the ways writing is typically done in these genres. Teachers can help students unpack difficult passages from a science textbook or social studies article by asking them to consider the author's rhetorical, generic, and grammatical choices. Students can then mimic these choices and strategies to write in content-specific genres. In this way, teachers can use writing activities to help students understand difficult reading assignments and use reading assignments as a springboard for writing activities.	**Science:** Write up your findings from the density experiment imitating the sentence structure of the professional lab report we studied in class. **Math:** Pick out the verb phrases in the following word problem. Now, put these phrases into your own words to identify which mathematical actions the problem is asking you to perform. **Social Studies:** Underline all the proper nouns and personal pronouns in your textbook's account of the colonial encounter. Who does the text suggest are the major players in this encounter? Do you agree? **Language Arts:** Identify the appeals to audiences in four recent campaign advertisements. Make a list of the most common appeals in these ads. **Music:** Find a review of a musical performance. Underline all of the evaluative/judgment terms. Now write a paragraph characterizing the writing strategies this author uses to communicate his or her opinion of a musical performance. *continued on next page*

A reproducible version of this chart can be found in online resources.

Table 4.1. Continued

Writing as Process	Examples
Many teachers say they use a "process" approach to writing instruction. Too often, however, the writing process is presented as a rigid step-by-step course of action. Teaching writing as a recursive process means providing students with opportunities to prewrite, draft, participate in peer review, revise, edit, and publish; however, it also means teaching students to be reflective, aware, and versatile writers. When students learn to monitor and modify their own writing processes, they will develop writing tools that they can apply to multiple writing situations, genres, and audiences. To become versatile and aware writers, students must encounter the writing process across the content areas; if students practice the writing process only in English class, they will not learn to apply those skills to other genres and content-area knowledges.	**Science:** Create a graphic organizer to represent the relationships between the key conclusions from your states of matter experiment. **Math:** Read over the word problems written by your writing workshop group. Write a peer-response letter to each group member, noting his or her use of mathematical vocabulary, clarity of ideas, and real-world applicability. **Social Studies:** Compose a one-page letter to accompany the final draft of your research essay. Describe the process you used to write this essay and note which aspects of the process went well and which were challenging. Place this reflection in your portfolio. **Language Arts:** Select a descriptive passage from the second draft of your literacy memoir. Working with your writing partner, revise the paragraph, making sure to include vivid verbs and figurative language. **World Languages:** Annotate your translation of Chapter 3 of *Don Quixote*. Why did your writing group choose a particular definition of a word? How did you handle figurative language or complex grammar structures?

best practices to invite these teachers into the writing initiative, for they will have been incorporating many of these practices into their classrooms already.

> **NCTE 4.2** *provides a reproducible version of this chart.*
>
>
>
> www.ncte.org/books/tiow

Professional development and training around content-area writing instruction can also help teachers identify and examine common problems in disciplinary writing. For example, in many classrooms students read one kind of text in class—such as a history textbook—and are asked to create another kind of text—such as a persuasive essay—for their writing assignments. This approach can make disciplinary writing expectations

Maximize Departmental Engagement with Best Practices in Content-Area Writing Instruction

- **Web-based PD**: NCTE offers sustained online professional development and Web seminars in content-area literacies.

- **Mini study groups**: Before the department meeting, have staff/faculty read an article about best practices in content-area writing instruction. The whole team can read the same article, or different articles can be assigned to individuals.

- **Policy briefs**: Present an NCTE policy brief (a summary of relevant research) to the staff. Teams can discuss how the research applies to their instructional practices.

- **School leaders**: Use your literacy coach, department leaders, writing leadership team, or outside experts to introduce best practices in content-area writing instruction.

mysterious for students because they don't have any models of what their own disciplinary writing should look like. However, if students learn how to analyze course readings and their own writing, using a tool such as functional grammar, disciplinary reading and writing expectations can become far more transparent. Encouraging your entire faculty to begin thinking about writing in their own disciplines, combined with quality professional development, will help surface many strategies for addressing content-area writing.

Analyze Student Writing

Analyzing student writing samples is a concrete way for departmental and grade-level teams to create a common starting point for the production of writing goals. Begin by asking each teacher to bring a manageable number of writing samples to the team meeting, perhaps two samples from three different students that span the range of writing abilities. Teachers may be concerned that their students' writing isn't strong enough or that their assignments are poorly written; remind them that the purpose of this exercise is not to evaluate their teaching, but to set the groundwork for important departmental and grade-level goal setting. Once the writing samples have been gathered and read, teams should begin to discuss the following questions:

- What do we think good writing looks like?
- What forms or genres are students most adept in?
- What genres do students struggle with?
- What are the similarities and differences between the genres that students read and those in which students write?
- Overall, what writing strengths do students have?
- What overall weakness do students have?
- How would we characterize the distance between the weaker writing samples and the stronger ones?
- Are students writing most successfully in any particular content area?
- Are they struggling in any particular content area?

NCTE 4.3 *offers these questions in survey form.*

www.ncte.org/books/tiow

Having a conversation around these questions and specific student texts will help to ensure that departmental and grade-level writing goals respond to the strengths and needs of your students. This does not mean you should lower your expectations of students or ignore the Common Core Standards; rather, examining student writing will help create a realistic picture of the school's strengths and challenges, so interventions can be targeted and growth is measurable.

Step 2: Support Grade-Level and Departmental Teams

As you know, instructional leaders cannot be at every meeting or in every classroom. To get your writing initiative off the ground, you will have to develop strong planning teams at the grade level and in the content areas. This is an excellent opportunity to give teams ownership over the writing initiative, encourage them to revisit their curricula, develop strong teamwork and new teacher-leaders, and communicate to your faculty/staff that you trust them to work autonomously.

Create effective planning teams.

Depending on the size of your school, planning teams may be divided differently. As you know, grade-level teams and content-area teams serve different purposes. At the beginning of a writing initiative, it is important to provide your faculty/staff opportunities to create writing goals

Strategies for Creating Team Planning Time

- Hold team meetings in place of faculty meetings once a month.
- Use gym periods, school assemblies, or music periods to create common preps.
- Use per-session pay to support after-school planning time.

within and across content areas. You'll also want to distribute leadership across the teams, mixing novice teachers with more experienced ones. Pay attention to which teams might need additional support, which might include a literacy coach, staff developer, learning specialist, or outside expert.

Build in adequate planning time to create and revisit goals.

To create a school culture that prioritizes writing, teachers need time to work together. Shared prep time will enable departments to determine which areas of writing instruction they plan to prioritize and allow grade-level teams to create common projects, a cohesive writing curriculum, and strategies for addressing the needs of individual students.

Help teachers make the most of planning time.

Successful teams work best under guiding principles. Ask members of each planning team to create their own guiding principles and then help the teams adhere to them. Guiding principles may include established meeting dates, time limits, established group roles (facilitator, note-taker, etc.), being prepared for meetings, and having a clear purpose. At this stage in the process, the purpose of team planning meetings will be to discuss best practices in content-area writing instruction, study student writing samples, create departmental and grade-level goals, and develop departmental benchmarks. Eventually, teams will begin to develop their own weekly purposes.

Step 3: Create Grade-Level and Departmental Writing Goals

Just like the schoolwide goals, departmental and grade-level goals must be collaboratively created and not imposed. It may be tempting—to save time or avoid conflict—to ask the literacy coach or a small group of teachers to create goals for teams; however, this deprives planning teams of opportunities to integrate the writing initiative with their tried-and-true approaches to content-area instruction. To capitalize on teachers' experience, create a common approach to writing instruction, and increase faculty/staff buy-in, it is important to give planning teams some autonomy. Team members can use the goal-setting model from the previous chapter (brainstorm, cluster, and prioritize) to create team goals or adopt another model of their own choosing. Goal setting is an ongoing and recursive process, especially when grade-level teams and content-area teams work simultaneously.

Grade-Level Goals

Grade-level writing goals will correspond with the schoolwide writing goals; however, these goals will focus on the individual learner. For example, if the school goal is to "implement authentic schoolwide writing assessment," a related grade-level goal might be: "Students will be able to write in a variety of genres for different audiences and different purposes." It is essential that every grade-level faculty/staff member feels able to contribute to each goal. This means that grade-level teams need to have some tough conversations. A common site of conflict has to do with the writing process. Content-area teachers may be uncomfortable teaching writing as a process or be concerned that it will detract from

Sample Grade-Level Goals

Students will be able to ...

1. Understand and use the writing process
2. Write in a variety of genres for different audiences and purposes
3. Engage in writing as a social process
4. Produce twenty-first century writing, using new media writing skills
5. Use writing as a tool to increase content learning

instruction time. The grade-level team will have to sort this out: perhaps the ELA teacher will conduct all writing minilessons, but each content-area class will have its own writers workshop; maybe each content-area teacher will teach one writing minilesson each week; perhaps the ELA teacher will incorporate content-area genres into his class and workshop essays that students are writing for other classes; maybe the literacy coach or a specialist will work with content-area classes to help support writing there. No matter how grade-level teams work out these tensions, every member should have a role to play in fulfilling team goals.

Content-Area Goals

Goal setting in the content areas is essential to the long-term success of a writing initiative. These goals will create consistency for students as they move from one grade to the next. They will also provide opportunities for faculty/staff to delve into the writing goals of their particular discipline. This is also a space where difficult conversations can emerge. A science teacher might insist that he prefers a worksheet for lab reports or a social studies teacher might argue that she wants students practicing the same writing genre all year. You will need to be open to these perspectives because these teachers have years of experience to suggest that worksheets or repeating writing genres *work* in their classes. Encourage teachers to work with their content-area teams to come up with a solution. Perhaps the science department should adopt the lab report worksheet as a prewriting activity to scaffold lab report drafts. Perhaps the biography that the social studies teacher assigns at the end of every unit could become a more informal, writing-to-learn activity built into every unit.

Create Curriculum-Appropriate Benchmarks

Once your planning teams have created content-area writing goals, you'll want to support them in creating benchmarks to help their students meet these goals. For these benchmarks to be meaningful, it is important that they be fully integrated into the existing curriculum. Some of your content-area teachers will have spent years creating effective curricula and lesson plans; it is best for your students, teachers, and school if the successful elements of a department's curriculum remain the same. If a school's content-area curriculum is strong, all of the skeletal elements can stay in place—the key is finding ways to incorporate best practices in writing instruction into the existing curriculum.

Sample Content-Area Goals

Students will be able to …

Social Studies

- Search, evaluate, and synthesize Web materials
- Gracefully integrate research into writing
- Write in multiple genres, including cause-and-effect essay, biography, research essay, and book review

Science

- Identify the generic, linguistic, and social features of science writing, including science journalism, reports, and poster presentations
- Draft, workshop, and revise lab reports
- Develop familiarity with write-to-learn activities such as marginal notes, diagrams, and summary

Math

- Reflect on mathematical process, thinking, and development
- Use the language of mathematics to express mathematical ideas precisely
- Identify the generic, linguistic, and social features of math writing, including word problems, proofs, poster presentations, and math journaling

English Language Arts

- Adjust use of written language (e.g., conventions, style, vocabulary) to communicate effectively with a variety of audiences and for different purposes
- Write every day for multiple purposes: to learn, to reflect, and to make connections between the classroom and the real world
- Master six invention techniques and develop metacognitive strategies for choosing how and when to use these techniques

Physical Ed/Health

- Develop familiarity with write-to-learn activities such as journaling, synthesizing, and note-taking
- Evaluate a variety of health-related informational sources for credibility and validity

Arts

- Critique examples of visual and performative art, using genre-specific vocabulary
- Develop familiarity with write-to-learn activities such as journaling and diagramming to reflect on visual and performative creative processes

World Language

- Draft, workshop, and revise translations in a variety of genres
- Use word-identification strategies, genre awareness, and organizational cues to translate passages

Examples of Curriculum-Appropriate Benchmarks

1. An eighth-grade social studies team decides that one of their goals is to have students practice writing in four authentic social studies genres. Next, they create four benchmarks that correspond with their existing curriculum. The first benchmark is, "students will draft, revise, and publish a book review," which nicely corresponds with a unit that emphasizes multiple perspectives on the Civil Rights Movement.

2. A team of eleventh-grade teachers decides that one of their goals is to have students "produce twenty-first century writing, utilizing new media writing skills." They may decide to work together to meet each benchmark. Their first benchmark might be, "introduce students to the basic concepts necessary for designing a webpage." In science, they might learn the basics of Dreamweaver. In math, they might learn a little about the mathematics behind computer programming. In social studies, they might talk about how to appropriately cite and/or link to images and texts from other sites. In visual art, students may learn the basics of visual design. In English language arts, students may analyze the possible audiences and rhetorical purposes for a range of webpages. The grade-level team's second benchmark might be, "students will draft a webpage based on their interdisciplinary inquiry project"; again, all content-area teachers would be involved in achieving this benchmark.

Integrating Specialists

When creating grade-level and content-area goals, it is essential to include the expertise of literacy, English language, and special education professionals in your school. These specialists often work with students in multiple grade levels and content areas, so they can be important links between classes and grade levels as teams create their goals. At the same time, it is important not to overschedule the time of these specialists. Many schools find it useful to have one specialist attached to one grade-level or content-area team for the entire year, even if they work with other students. This way, the planning team can draw from their expertise about struggling writers. No matter how you decide to include these specialists, it is essential that you acknowledge and use their expertise so that *all* students are included in the writing initiative.

Implementation Scenario: Supporting Writing in Content Areas

The regional education office in Iowa received expressions of concern from several instructional leaders in nearby schools. All claimed that student writing was not showing any improvement despite considerable investment in new materials and professional development for teachers in their English departments. In response the regional office suggested that extending writing instruction to all areas of the curriculum could address this problem, and it offered to provide a series of meetings for instructional leaders interested in strengthening content-area writing.

The instructional leaders attended the meeting, where they were introduced to materials and concepts similar to those included in this chapter. After the instructional leaders had become familiar with key concepts of content-area writing, they decided to launch writing-across-the-curriculum programs in their schools. As leaders kicked off programs in their individual schools, they maintained contact with one another, sharing ideas and suggestions and lending support as challenges emerged.

NCTE 4.4 *offers more examples of instructional leaders implementing principles from this chapter.*

www.ncte.org/books/tiow

Providing Professional Development

- Plan for long-term, context-specific professional development.
- Connect individual and whole-school development.
- Tap into internal and external resources.

Now that the schoolwide, grade-level, and department goals and benchmarks have been identified, this chapter will help you establish a well-developed system of long-term professional development that supports the writing initiative. As an instructional leader, you know you will need to be purposeful and thoughtful about how to plan across the school year. Your goal is to support teachers with regular, cohesive opportunities to continue their growth and development as writing teachers. You also recognize that few teachers may have had any course work in the teaching of writing, meaning that an array of professional development sources may be necessary.

Step 1: Use Key Principles for Basing Professional Development on Research and Best Practices

Principle #1: Schools with effective writing programs support long-term professional development conversations about writing.

Effective professional development is a long, ongoing process, which is one reason why it's important to enlist the support of stakeholders who will support the process. You've taken the right steps toward success by tapping into teachers' expertise and including them in shared decision making. And your schoolwide survey and goal setting have probably helped you determine common standards and expectations. Just know that you will also want to plan for the long haul—it can take a while to see lasting change:

- In schools with effective writing initiatives, school members are engaged in ongoing conversations about writing as important for learning and communication. This conversation may be interconnected with other initiatives and school goals—writing is an important way to support reading skills, link to the school community, and address equitable access.

- Effective writing initiatives demonstrate long-term planning and commitment over multiple years. This planning includes supporting ongoing intensive professional development and providing opportunities for feedback/revision of goals along the way.

Principle #2: Context-specific professional development supports schoolwide writing instruction.

Your comprehensive system of professional development (PD) should include a wide variety of opportunities best suited for your school. These opportunities should be crafted to help the school community achieve its schoolwide, grade-level, and departmental goals. The teachers at your school have already identified the needs at your specific site and have set goals in response to these needs.

According to research, this kind of buy-in is an important step in the right direction. Effective professional development relies on a rich mix of resources and a sensitivity to the school context. For writing initiative PD, this means taking into account teachers' philosophies of writing, allowing teachers to learn experientially and from one another, and making sure sessions are informed by research-based practices. Instructional leaders who exhibit strong knowledge of their school context and an interest in research-based writing practices better support their teachers in and out of the classroom.

Don't panic if you feel unsure at this point. Reading this book is a step in the right direction, and so is your attitude as a learner. What is important is that you avoid quick and easy answers that may not be based on best practices. Sure, anyone can purchase a one-size-fits-all program after using Google to search for "writing instruction," but this book will provide you with the resources to develop a long-term professional development plan that will be tied directly to your school's goals and linked to effective practice.

Example of Context-Specific Professional Development

Schoolwide goal: to integrate, support, and assess new media writing skills

Professional development activities:

- Learn how new media writing relates to student beliefs and identity.

- Read and respond to the new media writing of students and colleagues.

- Experience new media writing as a way of learning.

- Assess complete pieces of new media writing and study changes over time.

- Study new media writing in relation to multiple disciplines.

Cycle of Teacher Self-Evaluation

- Step 1: Teachers identify a problem or goal based on self-evaluation.
- Step 2: Teachers collect data.
- Step 3: Teachers conduct reflection and analysis of data.
- Step 4: Teachers initiate a plan for change, including the types of expertise/professional development needed to move forward. (They might also identify the need for guided professional development during steps 2 and 3 if this is a new process.)
- Cycle continues with steps 2–4.

Principle #3: Teacher evaluation (by self and leaders) should inform professional development opportunities.

Research shows that effective professional development is linked to teachers' reflective practice and self-evaluations. For instance, a cycle of self-evaluation can help teachers identify individual goals for improving their writing instruction and then create a plan for professional development.

And, of course, you will want to use your evaluations of teachers to help match them with the appropriate professional development opportunities (see Chapter 8 for more evaluation resources). Teachers who demonstrate weaknesses in a given area should be provided with professional development to move forward. One key resource for you as you provide feedback to teachers is to know where to find professional development opportunities.

NCTE 5.1 *offers a chart that links common teacher needs with professional development resources.*

www.ncte.org/books/tiow

Step 2: Create a Timely and Cost-Conscious Plan for Professional Development

As you know, professional development comes in many shapes and sizes. There are many different models and resources for writing-related professional development. Here's what you will need to do to create the most effective plan for your school:

- Provide **multiple opportunities** for professional development.
- Determine the best **balance of internal and external resources** for your school.
- Connect **individual and whole-school** professional development.
- Create **overall support structures** for all teachers as well as **new teacher support systems.**

Mark Your Calendar: Some Tips for Yearlong Planning

Before You Begin (March–July)

- Schedule outside consultants.
- Set aside professional development time for staff.
- Set aside time for class visits, laboratory, and small-group meetings.
- Create budget priorities for professional development opportunities.
- Fund and facilitate training for department heads and teachers in assessing student writing.

At the Start (August–September)

- Provide focused staff meetings to kick off the program.
- Review and revise this year's professional development plan.
- Develop institutional and schoolwide benchmarks to track progress.
- Predict problems in advance, and plan for how possible concerns provide ways to explore growth. For instance, you might predict that by mid-year, teachers will feel that student writing is not improving, that they are running out of time for writing instruction, or that individual students pose particular challenges. Design professional development sessions and benchmarks with possible problems in mind.

Mid-Year (October–March)

- Attend and send staff to NCTE's Annual Convention in November. This is a useful off-site activity for administrators and teachers that offers a broad range of professional development opportunities.
- Revisit and evaluate your plan with staff input: What is working well and what are the concerns? Are there underlying issues with the program, and if so, how many people in the school are experiencing the same concern? Use feedback to redesign professional development sessions and benchmarks.

At the Finish (April–June)

- Evaluate the strengths and weaknesses of the plan with staff input.
- Make revisions and begin planning for the next cycle of the program.

Options for Making It Happen

Next you'll find a variety of options for supporting the different aspects of improving writing at your school. There are two sections: (1) **on-site/internal professional opportunities** that focus on your current school resources, which are often the lowest budget options; (2) **off-site/external professional opportunities** with tips for how to get the most out of these options. Examples provided will help you determine the best combination for your school context and goals so you can create a professional development plan that aligns with the goals and context of your writing initiative.

Practical Ideas for Staff Meetings

There are many ways you can link activities in the whole-group meetings to what is happening in terms of individual and small-group development. Your staff can …

- Share what happened in peer classroom visits.
- Model what was learned on a school visit or at a conference.
- Work on their own writing to better understand what students are being asked to do.
- Reflect on writers' experiences and what this might imply for students.
- Experiment and practice with new technology.
- Discuss how a reading informs approaches to school goals.

On-Site/Internal Professional Opportunities

- *Whole-school workshops or meetings:* Some professional development opportunities should aim to bring together your entire faculty and staff to work on writing in your school. This schoolwide opportunity is a way to develop common language about the writing initiative. This will also provide a place to voice concerns and questions as you work to build a coherent program related to your schoolwide goals (see Chapter 3). Questions raised in these meetings should be broad enough to reach everyone: How do we make writing happen from grade to grade? How do we make sure we use a common language? How should we make budget decisions to best support the writing initiative? (What do we value—planning time, institutes, practical ideas, study group time, or other supports to make this happen?)

- *Professional books/resource sharing:* Summer reading is one way to launch new ideas with a staff. A well-selected text (traditional or online) can ensure that school members enter the conversation with a common language. Be sure to get recommendations from credible sources. (*See* **NCTE 2.3** *in Chapter 2 for online resources to help you select a book that matches well with your school's goals for the writing initiative.*)

- *Small groups or peer networks:* These groups can be cohorted study groups focused on a particular aspect of the writing goals or collaborative planning groups to align grade-level and/or departmental writing, like those discussed in Chapter 4. Case discussions also work well in these settings; in such discussions, a facilitator describes a challenging classroom scenario and the group brainstorms possible perspectives on the scenario before arriving at some resolution.

NCTE 5.2 *offers suggestions for leading a case discussion of student writing.*

www.ncte.org/books/tiow

- *Learning laboratory:* Often coordinated by a literacy coach or specialist, a small group (three to eight teachers) meets regularly. They work together on a regular basis in one lead teacher/literacy coach's class or laboratory. First, they help with and observe a sample lesson/activity. Afterward, they teach the lesson/activity in their own classes and meet to talk about their learning (both their struggles and their successes). This provides scaffolded, hands-on learning for teachers who are trying out new strategies, such as writers workshop, new media skills, or modeling techniques. Just as we expect our students to learn in authentic situations, this kind of professional development helps teachers actually apply new knowledge to their teaching contexts.

- *Peer classroom visits or peer coaching*: Cohorts of teachers can benefit from visiting one another's classes. For instance, in one professional development model teachers visit each other over a semester; at the end of the semester, teachers receive a compilation of two positive comments and two suggestions from each visiting teacher. These visits can help teachers participate knowledgeably in other small-group or schoolwide conversations as they try to answer questions such as, "What sorts of activities are helping students to become better writers? What struggles are teachers facing as they incorporate the initiative's goals into their classes?"

- *Internal consultants:* Look to the expertise already in your school. You may find that the literacy coach, reading specialist, or some classroom teachers will be able to provide inhouse consulting to meet your writing goals. However, you will want to plan ahead to reduce the teaching load to enable inhouse experts to serve as coaches or plan for staff meetings.

- *Internal teacher leadership:* Depending on the levels of expertise in your school, existing teachers may be a wonderful resource for other teachers, parents, or school volunteers. For example, they may be able to offer a course for new teachers or student teachers at lunch time, after school, or during classroom teaching. This requires freeing up existing teachers to provide mentorship time. Another example of internal leadership is to rotate teacher leadership within a small group. Each quarter, trimester, or unit, a new lead teacher could take on responsibilities for organizing materials for the current aspect of the initiative. The lead teacher would have privileges such as budget control, time to develop the team plan or attend outside development, and/or time to work with an outside expert.

Off-Site/External Professional Opportunities

- *School visits:* One option for professional development is to take a field trip. For example, teacher groups or the writing initiative leadership team can visit a school where writing workshops are effectively used. Try to visit a classroom that has a reputation for holding successful workshops and one that has typical struggles. Consider asking the following questions on your visit:

Tip: Don't think of off-site opportunities as simply something for your faculty and staff. Go along! Many instructional leaders find that attending professional development with teacher groups helps develop common language and goals. It also helps them understand their teachers' challenges and questions.

- Ask the principal: What seems to be going well in this classroom? What does this teacher struggle with? What do the students struggle with? How are you responding to these struggles?

- Ask the teacher: What writing skills are students learning in this classroom? What is helping them to learn? What issues do they continue to struggle with? How are you planning to respond to these struggles?

- Ask a student: Can you show me what you're working on today? Can you show me your writing folder/notebook? What is helping you to improve as a writer? What do you still struggle with?

NCTE 5.3 *offers more sample questions to ask on a school visit.*

www.ncte.org/books/tiow

- *Outside consultants:* While cost-conscious leaders use inhouse expertise, bringing in an expert from outside can provide vital expertise and fresh ideas. Explore the many types of consultants available to you: district consultants, private consultants, and university-based consultants. Everyone knows that outside consultants need to be selected carefully to have any long-term benefit. You will want to check references to make sure you can establish a fruitful consultant relationship. Consider the following tips for establishing productive relationships with outside consultants:

  - Use resources to find the best match between available consultants and your school's needs. If there is a site of the National Writing Project nearby, it may be able to help you find a local teacher consultant who meets your school's needs.

  - Plan ahead—as early as March for the following year.

  - Consider ways to provide enough time to establish a consistent approach. Using focused time before school starts and having a consultant work with your school in intervals throughout the school year can provide more long-term results than cramming information into a four-hour presentation. This means you will need to reserve dates on your school staff development calendar.

  - Mix face-to-face with online consultation to save money and time since you can fit a Web seminar or Skype session into a busy schedule more easily than a consultant visit. Furthermore, teachers benefit from interacting with consultants *after* they have tried out suggested strategies.

- *Institutes:* Several organizations offer institutes focused on writing. You can send teams of teachers to an institute that will help further your school/departmental goals. Institutes can also be a wonderful way for you to further your knowledge of writing and bond with your team.

NCTE 5.4 *lists NCTE consultants along with their areas of expertise.*

NCTE 5.5 *offers a list of institutes that foster professional development.*

www.ncte.org/books/tiow

Plan a School-Based Writing Institute: Institutes don't have to take place off-site. You can use an online source, such as NCTE's Pathways, to structure on-site learning.

Example Day One: Create a Common Perspective
a. **In the Large Group:** Learn about ways to teach writing.
b. **Individual:** Work through module on NCTE's Pathways.
c. **In Small Groups:** School members share reflections on their own writing. They practice writing methods together. For instance, teachers develop pieces that reflect their disciplinary expectations for students. Later, the pieces are used for modeling purposes in the teachers' classes.

Pathways offers sustained, intensive, and interactive professional development focused on hot-topic issues such as English language learners and twenty-first century literacies. Participants have access to Web seminars, podcasts, articles, live chats, classroom videos, and lesson plans in addition to the professional development modules.

Implementation Scenario: Homegrown Professional Development

Ike Thomas was the principal of a small high school in a rural area where there were few professional development opportunities available for teachers. The nearest college was more than two hours away, and the school district did not have funds to bring consultants to the school, but Ike was committed to improving student writing in his school. Before he became a principal, Ike had been the band director, and he drew on his experience as a musician in thinking about how he could provide professional development for the English teachers in his school. He remembered how he had helped students to improve by modeling how the instrument should be held and demonstrating how a passage should sound. He wondered if the school's teachers might be able to use a similar modeling technique to help students improve as writers.

From conversations with the faculty, Ike knew that few faculty members did any writing of their own, and none would describe themselves as writers. Near the end of the school year, Ike was able to find some unspent funds in his budget, and he offered interested teachers an opportunity to earn some extra money. The requirement was that they spend one week writing and sharing their work with one another. Then, later in the summer, they would be required to meet to plan ways of incorporating their experiences as writers into their teaching for the following year.

Although they initially expressed some reluctance, quite a few teachers agreed to Ike's plan, and after a week of writing and sharing, they all emerged with a new and powerful sense of themselves as writers. When they met to plan for the coming year, they agreed to share some of their own drafts with students and to draw directly on their experiences as writers in creating and responding to students' writing assignments.

NCTE 5.6 *offers more examples of instructional leaders implementing principles from this chapter.*

www.ncte.org/books/tiow

6

Structuring Institutional Support

- Address class size.
- Consider teacher assignment.
- Allocate technology.
- Reinforce key components of the writing initiative.

Once goals have been established and plans for professional development laid out, it is time to think about how you can create institutional support for the writing initiative. This chapter shows how you can address issues of class size, technology, writing across the curriculum, teacher assignments, evaluation, professional development, and the needs of diverse learners. As you know, schools across the country are facing budget crunches; nonetheless, you will still be making decisions about infrastructure that have an impact on the writing initiative. One of the most important things you can do as an instructional leader is to let instruction, in this case writing instruction, shape the infrastructure of your school rather than the reverse. It is easy to underestimate how much difference the strategic use of time, resources, and space can make. Creating schedules can seem like a completely routine task, but schedules can make an enormous difference in terms of teacher-to-teacher interactions. Decisions about school furniture or equipment can have a real impact on the quality of an instructional program. Even relatively small amounts of money can often make a significant difference in teacher development if used wisely. Assigning teachers to rooms can seem rather unimportant, but the relative proximity of teachers can make a significant difference in the quality of faculty interactions, which, in turn, has a powerful effect on student learning. With principles like these in mind, consider the specifics that follow.

Step 1: Address Class Size

Research shows that class size makes a significant difference in the effectiveness of writing instruction, and eighteen is the ideal number of students for a writing class. Best practices as described by the National Council of Teachers of English (see http://www.ncte.org/positions/statements/englishcoalitionsec) recommends that the teaching load for writing instructors be no more than four classes of twenty students. As you know, classes of eighteen students and teaching loads of fewer than one hundred students simply aren't possible in most schools. Instead of despairing about or dismissing completely the issue of class size, take a moment to consider the rationale behind these recommendations.

At the most fundamental level, recommendations about class size are based on the goal of ensuring that students will write regularly and receive sufficient individual attention to their writing. Students who write frequently and receive regular and thoughtful feedback on their writing will improve much more than those who write only occasionally and receive limited response to their writing. So while you hold smaller classes as a goal to be achieved when your school can afford it, you can focus on alternatives that provide more opportunities for students to receive feedback on their writing.

Encourage Peer Response

When teachers are well prepared to train students to become helpful readers of one another's writing, students can provide valuable responses to their peers' writing. Writing groups or writing workshops, as they are often called, do not work well unless teachers have learned how to prepare, monitor, and evaluate student participation. When you plan professional development opportunities for teachers to learn how to incorporate peer response into writing instruction, students in your school will receive more attention to their writing.

> **NCTE 6.1** *provides guidelines on establishing and using writing groups.*
>
>  **www**.ncte.org/books/tiow

Involve Parents and Community Members

If parents express interest in helping at your school, one way to involve them is to ask them to read and respond to student writing. This does not mean asking them to grade papers. Rather, they can serve as interested readers who address general issues such as what they found most interesting, what raised questions for them, and what they would like to know more about. Receiving responses like these can help students revise their writing and at the same time develop a greater understanding of audience needs. Parent volunteers do not need to be expert, or even experienced, writers to give students this sort of feedback; research suggests that students benefit from writing for a specific audience—the adults in your community are an important audience, no matter their level of writing expertise. If parents do not volunteer, you might consider building a relationship with members of a local service club, inviting them to serve as readers/responders. Or you might develop a partnership with a group of elders in your community. Regardless of their age or status, adults from the community can help compensate for less-than-ideal class sizes by providing a genuine audience for student writers.

Use Technology

Interactive Internet technologies such as Skype offer a low-cost way to provide students with an audience for their writing. This technology can facilitate conversations between students and community members, and it can also enable students to reach distant audiences such as students at another school, preservice teachers interested in working one-on-one with secondary school students, or other groups of adults. Colleges and universities often have an online writing lab (OWL), and you might consider building a relationship with a nearby institution to provide another audience for student writers in your school. Alternatively, you might use your own school's technological resources to establish a school-based OWL where more-skilled student writers can respond to the writing of their peers online.

NCTE 6.2 *offers guidelines for OWLs.*

www.ncte.org/books/tiow

Become an Audience Yourself

The most powerful thing you can do to foster a writing initiative is to pay close attention to student writing. Meeting occasionally with students and their teachers to look at a portfolio of student work, asking teachers to display student writing in your office, or inviting students to read excerpts of their writing at public meetings are all ways that you can become an audience for student writing in your school.

Step 2: Consider Assignment of Teachers

Research shows that teachers learn a great deal from one another, and one well-prepared teacher can make an enormous difference to a school or department. As you consider the assignments of teachers, you may want to consider questions such as the following:

- Which teachers have participated in professional development focused on writing?
- Which teachers regularly display student work that reflects writing achievement?
- Which teachers rank highest in your evaluation (see Chapter 8) of writing instruction?

When you have identified the teachers who are the most effective writing instructors, you may want to assign them to grade levels or instructional clusters where they can interact with less experienced or less skillful teachers since peer-to-peer influence can have dramatic influence on teacher improvement.

Thinking about teacher assignments also means considering how you use time and space. Arranging schedules so that a highly qualified teacher and a less able one share a planning period could foster exchanges that lead to improvements in the teaching of both. Similarly, considering where teachers are located in relation to one another can make a great difference in how experienced and beginning teachers interact.

Step 3: Evaluate Technology

Writing in the twenty-first century is linked directly to digital forms, and writing instruction in your school will be enhanced by whatever level of technological support can be provided. Access to technology remains uneven in U.S. schools. In 2005, for example, nearly 100 percent of public schools had access to the Internet, but student-to-computer ratios and access to broadband service was unevenly distributed. Furthermore, even when computers are available, they are often not used effectively or fully. Thinking strategically about the location of and access to computers and/or computer classrooms can make a great difference in the quality of writing instruction in your school.

Another dimension of access centers on the quality of technological resources. As you know, hardware and software do not always enhance instruction;

support personnel play a key role in making technology support teaching and learning. Dated equipment donated by a local business may seem like a tremendous resource until students find that the hardware and software are incompatible or that one or the other doesn't work anymore. Often, schools do not have staff to fix broken hardware or recommend appropriate software; this is another case where reaching out to your school and local community can have a tremendous impact on the success of your writing initiative. Perhaps community volunteers have the expertise required to acquire and maintain software. Some schools have trained a team of students to maintain equipment, giving students valuable exposure to technology.

Even when equipment is working effectively, other challenges complicate its use. It is impossible to overestimate the importance of thinking systematically about the scheduling of computers since they are so frequently underused. In 2005, the average time a student spent using a school computer was twelve minutes a week. Many schools already have a schedule of computer lab or laptop cart usage. However, such schedules are not always responsive to instructional needs; the computers are often used in the final stages of a writing project merely for typing. Consider having each departmental and grade-level team map out a schedule for sustained computer use that stems from curricular plans.

Teachers need professional development support to integrate technology into writing instruction. As the emergence of Web 2.0 shows, social networking is an integral part of students' use of technology outside of school, and effective writing instruction will incorporate this dimension. For teachers, however, this means learning to use new technologies and adopting new pedagogical practices, both of which will require focused professional development. The benefit of investing your time and energy in this endeavor is that integrating technology and writing instruction can support students' academic success in all content areas.

Step 4: Reconsider Key Factors in the Writing Initiative

Writing in All Subjects

Even when teachers in all subjects have helped to create goals for writing as described in Chapter 4, it is likely that you will find some resistance to teaching writing in all subjects. Part of your responsibility will be to assure all stakeholders that writing is part of the infrastructure of the school and that it is essential to student learning.

You can encourage writing in all subjects by making it clear that this is one of your priorities. You can also model the importance of writing in all areas by showing that writing is important in your own work. Commenting on your own processes of writing, sharing the challenges you face as a writer, and explaining how you overcome them can go a long way toward convincing teachers that they should integrate writing into all subjects.

Effective Evaluation

High-stakes tests have become part of evaluation, and it does not serve teachers or students well to ignore that fact. The scores that students receive on timed writing tests can have a powerful effect on your school as well as on the lives of individual students. Faced with this situation, some instructional leaders reach for canned writing programs or quick fixes, but they are nearly always disappointed in the results.

Studies show that students who participate in a coherent and well-developed program of instruction do well on state-mandated writing assessments, even if they have not spent months preparing for the test. As an instructional leader, you can encourage teachers to follow best practices in writing instruction, assuring them that students who learn strategies for writing, write regularly, and receive useful feedback on their work will do well on a high-stakes test.

Taking this stance enables you to direct teacher attention toward more effective evaluation that supports instruction. Among the things that can be evaluated are portfolios of student work and revisions completed over time. Evaluating features such as demonstrations of audience awareness and evidence offered to support an argument can help teachers and students alike to understand where instruction needs to be strengthened or modified.

Using Portfolios

Many schools have found portfolios to be useful in supporting student writing. Here are some of the general steps to developing portfolios, whether they are e-portfolios or traditional paper portfolios:

1. Determine which kinds of informal and formal pieces of writing will reflect student learning in a course (or across content areas for a grade level).

2. Set deadlines for informal pieces and a series of drafts for formal pieces.

3. Structure reflection opportunities for students to track their strengths, goals, and areas for improvement with each piece.

4. Create rubrics for major portfolio pieces and/or the final portfolio.

---

5. Determine compilation procedures: Are these electronic portfolios housed on the server? Will students compile pieces in a folder in the classroom or a binder? How long will portfolios be stored at the school and where?

6. Consider uses of the portfolio that extend beyond evaluation: Will you use the portfolios for conferences with parents/guardians? Can they be used for high school, college, or job applications? Will you evaluate them in relation to the writing initiative?

Effective evaluation uses writing rubrics or scoring guides that specify criteria for writing quality, not simply quantity. Writing assignments can be aligned with the goals of your school's program of instruction, and rubrics can reflect these goals. Among the features of effective evaluation are the following:

- Allow for choice between several writing prompts to reduce the risk of evaluating students on the basis of their cultural knowledge rather than their writing proficiency.

- Use writing assignments that help students reflect on their current understandings, questions, and learning processes.

- Focus on both summative writing where students can show what they have learned and informal writing-to-learn to help increase student learning of content materials.

- Allow students a choice in writing tasks and genres to improve motivation.

- Avoid writing assignments that are not readily understood by people who come from various cultural backgrounds.

Good rubrics not only contribute to accurate, authentic assessment, but they can also enhance student learning by helping to guide revision and improvement, by helping students begin to identify the features of good writing, and by helping students begin to see patterns of strength and weakness across assignments. Rubrics also encourage self-reflection and self-assessment, skills crucial for teaching students to be versatile, twenty-first century writers. Excellent rubrics should:

- Articulate a clear criteria for assessing writing based on observable features (e.g., "all examples and quotations are effectively chosen, integrated, and developed; each reference is properly cited")

- Ask students to assess their own work

- Make apparent strategies for improvement
- Use vocabulary and writing-specific terminology that students are familiar with
- Align with the appropriate grade-level standards, writing genre, student knowledge, and learning goals

Many schools create a common rubric based on a combination of writing initiative goals, the Core Common Standards, and students' instructional needs. It is recommended, however, that this rubric is modified by departmental/grade-level teams for specific writing assignments; this way, the rubric aligns with both the larger goals of the initiative and the specific skills that students are learning in a particular unit. Table 6.1 is a sample essay rubric that you might use as a model for creating your own schoolwide rubric.

Professional Development

As Chapter 5 explained, professional development will be an essential part of a writing initiative, and as you consider the various forms of institutional support necessary for the writing initiative, it is worth keeping in mind the strategies that Chapter 5 suggested for creating an infrastructure to support professional development: plan time for professional development throughout the year, not just at the beginning of the initiative; use time in-school and out-of-school for PD opportunities; find creative ways to carve out time for whole staff/faculty meetings, as well as departmental and grade-level meetings; encourage schoolwide commitment to make good use of everyone's time.

Diverse Learners

The infrastructure of your school is probably already calibrated to accommodate the needs of students with special needs. In thinking about a writing initiative, it is important to consider how adjustments can be made so that teachers can give these students the attention they need to succeed as writers. Ideally, class size will be reduced for populations of diverse learners. In addition, this is an area where professional development can pay dividends in student learning. In particular, teachers can benefit from professional development that prepares them for collaborative teaching arrangements where they work with specialists in ELL or learning disabilities to help all students become better writers. One wonderful aspect of a writing initiative is that it can help teachers talk more explicitly about the academic expectations for writing (and reading) for all students.

Table 6.1. Sample Essay Rubric

Category	Exceptional	Commendable	Adequate	Some Achievement	Little Evidence of Achievement
Purpose	has a clear, specific, original purpose that matters to a wide audience	has a clear, specific purpose; strives to say something original to a wide audience	has a clear purpose, which may not be original; may be too specific or too general	has an unclear or unfocused purpose	has no clear purpose
Evidence and Development	specific examples are effectively chosen, integrated, and developed; each reference is properly cited	overall strong use of examples; integration, choices, or development may be ineffective at times; each reference is properly cited	includes examples; they may not be fully developed or integrated; each reference is properly cited	includes examples, but doesn't integrate or develop them; each reference is properly cited	argument is unsupported; references may not be cited or cited improperly
Organization and Clarity	organization is innovative and clear; each paragraph clearly supports the purpose	organization is clear; all paragraphs support the purpose; may have minor inconsistencies or lack originality	organization breaks down at certain points; all paragraphs may not clearly support the purpose	organization detracts from effectiveness of the paper; many paragraphs may not support the purpose	there is no clear organization or structure
Language Use	varies structure, length, and complexity of sentences, and displays command of lucid and elegant vocabulary	sentences are varied and easy to read; diction is sophisticated without being forced	sentences are easy to understand but lack verve; diction may be inconsistent; some words are misused or overly used; wordiness could be reduced	sentences are difficult to understand and word choice is weak; tone is inappropriate for the purpose and/or sentences are needlessly wordy	demonstrates no effort to match sentence structure, tone, and level of diction to the subject matter or the audience
Conventions	writing is free of grammatical and mechanical errors; essay is professionally presented	occasional grammatical or mechanical error does not impede the argument of the essay; essay is professional	some mechanical and grammatical problems; essay is semi-professional	grammatical and mechanical errors impede the argument of the essay; essay is semi-professional	mechanical or grammatical errors interfere with meaning; not professional

Implementation Scenario: Addressing Class Size

Garfield Middle School was overcrowded, and class size continued to grow as Garfield attempted to accommodate more and more students, many of whom were recent immigrants. This growth in size and increase in the number of English language learners came at the time when Joan Moore, the literacy coach, was trying to help teachers prepare students to do better on the state-mandated writing test. Joan knew that teachers simply didn't have time to respond to the writing of their 175 students, but she also knew that the only way to help students learn to write better was to give them opportunities to write regularly. Joan worked with teachers to set up two programs that would give students opportunities to write regularly for responsive audiences.

The first, the American Voices program, required all students in the school to interview parents or guardians about when they, or their ancestors, came to the United States and write an account of this arrival. Parents/guardians were encouraged to write a translation of the student's story in the language of their country of origin. This project included developing and practicing interview questions, writing multiple drafts of the account, and ultimately producing the final account, often in two languages. For the culminating activity, parents/guardians were invited to their student's class and each pair read their account for the class.

The second project extended across the entire school year and involved members of the local Rotary Club coming to school every Friday, where they met in the gym with small groups of students to listen to students read their writing aloud. The Rotarians were not expected to evaluate the writing, but Joan gave them a list of issues they might comment on, including what they found most interesting, what wasn't clear, and what they would like to know more about. Even though the Rotarians didn't offer corrections, Joan noticed that some students started editing and rethinking their writing because they were able to recognize problems or form new ideas when they read to another person.

NCTE 6.3 *offers more examples of instructional leaders implementing principles from this chapter.*

www.ncte.org/books/tiow

Sustaining and Improving a Writing Initiative

This section contains tools instructional leaders can use in assessing a school writing program and evaluating individual teachers. The chapters in this section also offer strategies for addressing student learning and ensuring sustainability for a school writing program.

Chapter 7: Assessing of Student Learning

- Assess student learning.
- Re-survey students.
- Determine ongoing writing goals.

Chapter 8: Evaluating and Recruiting Teachers

- Use multiple types of observation.
- Acknowledge teacher expertise.
- Support teachers with professional development.
- Consider writing expertise during the hiring process.

Chapter 9: Conducting Programmatic Assessment

- Support regular opportunities for program assessment.
- Promote end-of-year programmatic assessment.

- Survey and improve institutional resources and professional development.

- Survey and revise instructional support and professional development.

Appendix
Apply for NCTE Certification of Excellence for Writing Initiative

7

Assessing Student Learning

- Support assessment of student writing.
- Re-survey students' attitudes and beliefs about writing.
- Determine ongoing writing goals based on assessment and survey results.

Because the purpose of the writing initiative is to improve student writing, evaluation of this program should begin at the student level. How have students' writing skills changed throughout the implementation of the writing initiative, and what areas of concern remain? This chapter provides a variety of techniques for assessing student learning and for using these assessments to improve instruction. It also provides an end-of-year student survey similar to survey 1.4, which will allow you to compare students' attitudes about writing from then to now. These resources can help you track student progress throughout the school year. Finally, this chapter offers suggestions for determining ongoing writing goals based on assessment and survey results.

Step 1: Assessing Student Learning

Crucial to sustaining and improving a writing program is having concrete methods and procedures for evaluating student writing. Frequent assessment of student writing, both formal and informal, is important because it provides teachers with feedback that can help them adjust their instruction depending on students' needs, and it provides students with feedback on how their writing skills are developing. Because the writing initiative includes both schoolwide and department-specific writing goals and benchmarks, it will be important to make time for teachers and instructional leaders to collaborate within and across disciplines as they evaluate student learning and revise writing goals. Teachers should be encouraged to use a variety of formative and summative assessment measures in their classrooms, and to track student progress within grade-level, departmental, and schoolwide contexts.

Using Formative Assessments

Formative assessments are measurements for learning purposes. These are frequent, informal assessments that can help both teachers and students reflect on progress and adjust writing instruction and foci accordingly. Next are several examples of formative assessments as well as suggestions for when and how they might be used. This is not an exhaustive list, nor is it meant to be prescriptive. However, given the variety of writing skills, goals, and types of learners in a given classroom, it is essential that teachers and instructional leaders have myriad assessment techniques and create assessment-friendly classrooms.

Observation
Effective writing instructors observe students during their writing processes, looking for signs and patterns of creativity, struggle, and competency. Encourage teachers to pay attention to students' interests and attitudes as well as the writing behaviors they display. This kind of assessment helps teachers understand where students are and how to scaffold next steps.

Short Writing Tasks
Students should have multiple opportunities to write in every classroom. Writing instructors can use these opportunities to assess students' understanding of subject content (writing to learn) as well as specific writing skills that are being currently addressed.

Drafts
While writing instructors will likely read and grade final drafts of writing assignments, they can skim or read partial drafts to help students as they develop their ideas. Drafts can be collected as homework assignments or discussed in whole-class revision sessions. Assessment of drafts enables instructors to understand better where students are at different stages of writing and learning.

Conferences
Conferencing is an excellent way for teachers to work one-on-one with students to provide student-specific instruction and feedback. Conferences can be 5- to 10-minute sessions that happen during class writing time. Alternatively,

students can form two- to three-person peer revision groups to discuss current writing projects, and writing instructors can observe these groups. Conferencing enables teachers to understand how individual students are engaging with the material and writing. Conferencing also helps students gauge their strengths and areas for improvement as they converse with their peers, instructors, or other authentic audiences.

Using a Variety of Summative Assessments

Summative assessments are measurements of learning. These are infrequent, formal assessments designed to examine student achievement based on curricular and school writing standards. Below are several examples of summative assessments as well as suggestions for when and how they might be used. Again, this list is not meant to be exhaustive but rather to reinforce the multiple-assessment approach to student writing.

End-of-Unit Writing Assignments

Students can write in multiple, real-world genres to demonstrate content knowledge and writing competency. Formal lab reports, literary analyses, research papers, and multigenre assignments should reflect content material, students' interests, and departmental writing goals. This kind of assessment is useful for determining whether students can apply in-depth learning in authentic situations.

Portfolios

Writing portfolios allow students and instructors to track writing progress throughout the year. Portfolios provide the ability to assess students' informal and formal writing assignments in various genres, as well as student reflections on how their writing skills and processes have changed over the year. Instructors can collect portfolios at the end of each unit or semester in order to have longitudinal writing samples from each student. This kind of long-term picture of student writing can help instructors see how students have met goals for college readiness.

NCTE 7.1 *outlines the steps necessary to establish portfolio evaluation.*

www.ncte.org/books/tiow

Standardized Tests

Throughout middle school and high school, students will probably be required to take several state- or district-mandated writing assessments. The results from these tests can help writing instructors determine how school writing goals compare to national and state standards, how writing instruction can be tailored to meet a variety of expectations, and how students can be better prepared for multiple writing tasks.

Measuring Student Achievement Using Multiple Assessments

The most important part of any writing initiative is the effect it has on student learning. Standardized test scores or high-stakes tests based on a single piece of timed writing are, of course, measures, but, as the data gathered at the beginning of this initiative showed, student writing abilities can be measured in several ways, and these tests are only one form. Other useful measures include standardized interviews or focus groups; direct measures of untimed writing produced using a process; and collections or portfolios of student writing. This section explains each.

Scores on Writing Tests

Longitudinal comparison of scores achieved on the same measure of writing ability by all students in your school will provide a general overview of student achievement, but it will not provide much information on the specific skills students have or have not developed.

Targeted comparison of scores achieved on the same test by specific populations in your school can provide useful information about various subgroups of students. Learning, for example, how the performance of English language learners compared with that of native speakers in the tenth grade can inform instruction. Similarly, comparisons of scores achieved by male and female students can provide helpful information for teachers. Throughout your assessment of the writing initiative, it will be important that you not only consider how the initiative has gone overall but also whether it has served your entire student population; the information you gather from a targeted comparison is an important first step. From here, you will have to introduce new instructional and institutional interventions to support student subgroups. In this way, high-stakes tests can be used to improve instruction, helping particular subgroups of students learn to write not only for tests but also for multiple purposes and audiences.

Detailed analysis of specific dimensions of test scores can generate valuable suggestions for future planning. Determining, for instance, the areas where a majority of students encountered difficulty on the test or identifying areas where students performed especially well can guide instruction.

Direct Measures of Student Writing

Common prompts used by all teachers at a given grade level will produce specific information about strengths and weaknesses in student writers, as well as an indication of their general level of accomplishment. Common prompts can also produce crucial information about how students engage the writing process, because they can respond to the prompt over a period of time. Such an approach is not only a more accurate assessment of students' writing skills, but it is also more equitable, appealing to a wide range of learning styles. If grade-level groups of teachers gather to evaluate the student writing together, their meetings can foster professional development at the same time that it provides a measure of student competency that goes beyond what a timed writing test produces.

Student Work Samples

Portfolios, either electronic or paper versions, or other collections of student work can provide in-depth perspectives on student achievement. The process of creating a work sample develops metacognitive capacities in students because it requires them to reflect on their own work. Assessment of a school's writing program does not require detailed examination of every student's work sample or portfolio. Rather, you can select a representative sample from each grade level and focus analysis on these to determine how well students are writing.

> **NCTE 7.2** *offers a process for analyzing student work samples or portfolios.*
>
>
> **www.ncte.org/books/tiow**

Step 2: Re-survey Students

In addition to assessing students' writing progress, it is also important to consider whether students' beliefs about and attitudes toward writing have changed over the year. Effective writing programs encourage students to see themselves as competent and lifelong writers, and to make connections between curricular and extracurricular writing practices. Therefore, it is important to consider the ways students' writing competencies and attitudes have or have not changed over the course of the year. Note also that students' and teachers' perceptions of the writing program may vary in significant and important ways. To create a fuller picture of the writing initiative, it is therefore necessary to obtain teachers' and students' opinions. Questions such as the following represent the types that can provide a student perspective on the writing initiative:

- Has writing instruction changed this year and, if so, in what ways?
- Have your writing skills improved this year? If so, how? If not, why do you think they haven't?
- What kinds of connections do you see between your out-of-school and your in-school writing?
- If you could improve one aspect of writing instruction in your school, what would it be?

NCTE 7.3 *Provides a survey that can be used with students.*

www.ncte.org/books/tiow

In analyzing the surveys, look for common answers and patterns among students' responses. If possible, you can compare students' individual surveys with their responses from survey 1.4. Teachers and instructional leaders may want to consider the following questions: Do students perceive changes in the ways writing is taught and assessed across classrooms? Do students feel as though their writing skills have improved? How do students' perceptions of the writing initiative and their own achievement compare with teachers' perceptions of the writing initiative and evaluation of students' writing?

Step 3: Determine Ongoing Writing Goals

The classroom assessments, teacher collaboration sessions, and students' surveys can help instructional leaders and teachers to determine which benchmarks are or are not being met, and to revise ongoing writing goals. If, for example, the data indicate that students need further instruction in writing for standardized tests or writing for a variety of audiences, curricular and pedagogical choices can be made accordingly. Schoolwide and departmental writing goals should respond to the needs of students and teachers and should be frequently revisited.

Implementation Scenario: Detailed Analysis of Test Results to Inform Instruction

Student scores on the state-mandated writing test for a middle school in Michigan had been among the lowest in the county for several years. When test results were reported the next year, Kanya White, the principal, asked the eighth-grade teachers to join her in looking at student performance in more detail to determine instructional needs. With assistance from the district's assessment experts, Kanya and the teachers looked at the subscores for each eighth grader in the school. Together they were able to determine that students had particular difficulty with using varied sentence types and providing sufficient detail.

With this information, Kanya encouraged the teachers to develop instructional units that introduced students to multiple sentence types and gave them opportunities to develop ideas in writing. The teachers, in response, identified and taught several strategies for sentence expansion and variation, including distinguishing sentence types and writing cumulative sentences. The teachers also identified questions about audience and purposes for writing that could be used to help students develop ideas; requested funding to participate in a Web seminar on establishing peer response groups; and developed a schoolwide rubric that emphasized the development of ideas.

NCTE 7.4 *offers more examples of instructional leaders implementing principles from this chapter.*

www.ncte.org/books/tiow

8

Evaluating and Recruiting Teachers

- Observe teachers.
- Acknowledge teacher expertise.
- Connect teachers to resources.
- Consider writing expertise during hiring process.

Now that you have considered ways to support assessment of student writing and to shape ongoing writing goals, you can apply this knowledge to your ongoing teacher evaluation and recruitment practices. This chapter includes a guide for observing teachers with an eye toward helping them improve as teachers of writing, as well as resources for addressing teacher needs. It also includes writing-oriented questions to consider when hiring new teachers.

Step 1: Use Multiple Types of Observations

Using multiple types of observation can help you evaluate strengths and needs related to your school's writing initiative. Some observations will include teachers observing one another in order to spur self-evaluation and cross-disciplinary thinking. In others you can focus on specific aspects of writing instruction with a new or experienced teacher or gain a sense of how departmental goals are progressing.

Walk-Through

You are probably familiar with this technique of visiting classes for a few minutes at a time, focusing on particular areas to observe. Walk-throughs work best when teachers don't see them as punitive and have a chance to collaborate with observers about the walk-through focus. As an instructional leader, you can walk through multiple classes based on a goal-related focus and share findings across multiple departments. It can be helpful to have a focus question for the week, such as "How are students using writing to learn in each subject?" or "What are the visible reading/writing connections in our classrooms?" Walk-throughs can also be a useful way to value teacher expertise and share with others. For instance, you and less experienced teachers could share walk-through observations of classes with an experienced writing teacher.

Displays of Student Writing

In addition to classroom observations, instructional leaders can learn about teachers' effectiveness by noting public displays of student writing, by examining student work samples, or by observing students writing outside the classroom. In this case, you will want to focus on highlighting positive examples rather than taking a punitive stance toward teachers who do not have displays.

Focused Observation Based on Teachers' Self-Evaluation or a Schoolwide Goal

Chapter 5 emphasized the importance of teachers' self-evaluations for their professional learning. While conducting focused teacher evaluations, you can involve teachers in the process and ask them to set observation goals, most likely based on the departmental or schoolwide goals. Teachers can respond to a list of preobservation questions prior to a focused observation.

> **NCTE 8.1** *offers a reproducible copy of preobservation questions.*
>
>
> www.ncte.org/books/tiow

Using questions such as those in the following list can enable you to provide affirmation for what's going well and support the ongoing learning of the teacher.

Teacher:	Class:	Date:

Schoolwide/Departmental Writing Goals
- What learning and teaching activities will be observed?

- What do you want students to take away from the lesson? For subject area? As writers?

- Is there anything in particular that you want to be focused on during the observation?

- How will you know if students have learned during this lesson?

- Do students have any particular needs or characteristics that the observer should know about?

- What else will we need to discuss?

Overall Guide for Observing Teachers

Student achievement is the ultimate measure of teacher quality. It is important to recognize that student achievement may vary depending on students' writing abilities and needs; teachers should not be penalized for working with struggling writers. Accordingly, each of the following questions, which draws on a principle that characterizes effective writing instruction, is framed in terms of students' knowledge and behavior. These principles will also support your goals to meet national standards in writing. Observations of a classroom with a highly effective teacher of writing would yield all answers in the affirmative. Content-area teachers—who are teaching and using writing in their subject area—will be more effective by incorporating these strategies.

- Do students write every day?

- Is the use of copying in writing limited?

- Do students keep journals or participate in other types of informal writing?

- Do students exhibit familiarity with many forms or genres of writing, especially those related to this subject area?

- Do students express confidence about their abilities as writers in this subject area?

- Do students use writing as a way of learning in this subject area?

- Do students have opportunities to see teachers model their own writing in this subject area?

- Do students refer to writing strategies used by authors whom they have read?

- Do students write for authentic audiences?

- Do student use computers for writing and gathering information?

- Do students demonstrate ability to distinguish between reliable and unreliable sources of information on the Internet?

- Do students demonstrate knowledge of multiple strategies for generating ideas for writing?

- Do students share their writing in progress with one another?

- Do students participate in brief individual writing conferences with their teachers?

- Do students exhibit ability to comment constructively on the writing of their peers?

- Do students show that they can distinguish between revising (conceptualizing or rethinking a piece of writing) and editing (correcting errors in spelling, punctuation, and sentence structure)?

- Is student writing displayed in the classroom or in class publications, either on paper or online?

- Do students demonstrate understanding of the criteria used to evaluate their formal writing?

- Can students construct a rubric or scoring guide to evaluate writing?

What is . . .

an improvement portfolio? The teacher compiles information (post-observation conversations, strategies, etc.) to improve an area related to his or her writing instruction and writes an analysis of improvement or areas for future teaching changes.

an instruction-based project? The teacher identifies a change that needs to occur to improve student learning, works with instructional leaders to develop an action plan, and writes an analysis of the project's effectiveness.

As you know, teacher evaluations should rely on multiple instruments. Beyond observations, sources to help you answer the above questions might include video-recordings, student feedback, parent/guardian feedback, improvement portfolios, or an instruction-based project. In addition, it can be valuable to ask teachers to do a self-evaluation like the one in Table 8.1.

Step 2: Acknowledge Teacher Expertise

As you conduct observations, you will begin to see teacher strengths and areas of growth. Part of supporting overall teacher learning will be to affirm what you are seeing. A key affirmation strategy is to acknowledge teacher expertise. One way to do this is to write a quick note after a walk-through or after seeing student writing displayed.

Table 8.1. Teacher Self-Evaluation Worksheet

	Schoolwide Writing Goals	Departmental Goals
What are your individual goals in relation to the larger goals?		
Progress on goals:		
Resources you need:		
Strengths you can share:		
Possible goal for next year:		

Dear Ashley,

Thanks so much for inviting me into your classroom today. I've never seen students so excited about writing in learning logs. It is clear that they are understanding the important ways that writing can help them understand key concepts, "just like scientists," as you said in class! I'd love to hear more about how you decided on this assignment and what questions you have. Overall, this seems like something we should share with the whole department!

Thanks again,

Your Instructional Leader

If you choose to make teacher expertise public, choose carefully to highlight someone who is achieving success based on one of the goals. One strategy is to choose a teacher (probably not a beginning teacher) who may not be a usual leader and who may not have been the first to volunteer for the initiative. By affirming this teacher, you can solidify buy-in to the initiative while also helping other teachers learn about an effective strategy.

Step 3: Support Teachers with Professional Development as Part of the Evaluation Process

Part of your role as an instructional leader in the writing initiative will be to match teachers who show they have needs with resources to support their learning. You can match common teacher needs with resources provided through NCTE or recommended as part of this book.

As you start evaluating teachers, it is a good time to remind yourself that this is a long-term initiative. As you know, the more you can approach evaluation

Table 8.2. Matching Teachers' Needs with NCTE Professional Resources (sample table)

Teacher Needs	Research Policy Briefs	Pathways Program	Other Resources
Help integrating writing into content area	Adolescent Literacy	Advancing Adolescent Literacy Pathway: How can I support my students as readers/writers while teaching challenging content? Web Seminar: Writing in Every Content Area	Learning resources: Content Literacy
Ideas for how to help students write more and in different formats, including new media	21st Century Literacies	21st Century Literacies Pathway: Re-seeing Writing Process with Blogging	NCTE Definition of 21st Century Literacies *Teaching Writing Online: How and Why* (Scott Warnock, NCTE, 2009)
To know more about kinds of writing instruction that will help all students on standardized tests	English Language Learners Writing Now What We Know: Assessment	Teaching and Learning with English Language Learners Pathway Advancing Adolescent Literacy Pathway	*Writing on Demand* (Leila Christenbury, Anne Ruggles Gere, and Kelly Sassi, Heinemann, 2005) NCTE Beliefs about the Teaching of Writing

in supportive, collaborative ways, the more you will be able to encourage lasting effects. When teachers feel they have choices, they are likely to respond to your feedback. It can help to ask teachers after the observation to identify areas where they need additional resources. Then, you can use this book and online resources to help match them with appropriate resources.

Table 8.2 shows how you can offer professional development suggestions as part of the evaluation process. For instance, the chart shows resources that might be useful to a teacher based on the needs identified during the evaluation process.

> **NCTE 8.2** *offers an expanded chart with further examples*
> www.ncte.org/books/tiow

Step 4: Consider Writing Expertise during the Hiring Process

Given the inevitable faculty turnover, there will probably be opportunities to hire new faculty as the writing initiative proceeds. Hiring can be an opportunity to add new expertise in writing to the faculty.

Questions for Hiring Writing Instructors

While these questions focus primarily on the hiring of writing instructors, they are equally applicable for hiring candidates in all disciplines, because the writing initiative depends on writing receiving attention in every classroom. Furthermore, while underresourced schools can have a difficult time recruiting experienced teachers, this list can help you select strong candidates will add crucial writing expertise to your faculty. It is, of course, impossible to predict how successful any prospective teacher will be in the classroom, but the combination of scanning a candidate's transcript for a course on the teaching of writing, viewing (when available) video clips of the candidate teaching writing, and asking questions that touch on the topics below can help identify the most promising applicants.

- **Writing Processes.** Nearly all applicants will claim to approach writing as a process, but probing for details about implementation, including teaching strategies for developing ideas, creating a draft, and, especially, revising and editing the draft, will reveal the applicant's depth of knowledge.

- **Reading-Writing Connection.** Effective writing instructors will explain that reading provides strategies and other resources for writers.

- **Multiple Forms.** Students need to write in many different genres—letters, essays, stories, poetry, and blogs, for example—and they need opportunities for **informal** (low-stakes and impromptu) as well as **formal** (composed over time and graded) writing. A promising candidate will be able to describe several possible assignments that include this range.

- **Connection between Instruction and Assessment.** Effective teachers can explain how an assignment leads to classroom activities that support student writers and how, in turn, the evaluation of writing is linked to assignments and further growth in writing.

- **Use of Technology.** Writing in the twenty-first century is directly tied to new media, and research shows that students are more engaged with learning when they use technology. Effective instructors will be able to describe how they integrate technology into their teaching.

- **Writing and Learning.** Research shows that writing aids learning in all disciplines, and a promising applicant will be able to explain how formal and informal writing help students learn.

NCTE 8.3 *offers an interview protocol that highlights these issues.*

www.ncte.org/books/tiow

Implementation Scenario: Communicating Schoolwide Goals during Interviews

The writing initiative at an Illinois high school developed common rubrics that were used across the entire curriculum, with adaptations to suit disciplinary needs and specific assignments. Kendra Grady, the principal, wanted to be sure that new teachers would be able to support and help with the continued reshaping of the rubric. During interviews with applicants for all subjects, Kendra asked questions based on the interview protocol of NCTE 8.3.

If candidates were able to answer these questions satisfactorily, Kendra asked them to describe how they had used rubrics to evaluate writing in the past and then shared the schoolwide rubric with candidates, requesting them to explain how they might use the schoolwide rubric to foster student learning. This enabled Kendra and her colleagues to determine how applicants would approach writing instruction, and it also ensured that the schoolwide goals of writing improvement were on the table from the beginning.

NCTE 8.4 *offers more examples of schools implementing principles from this chapter.*

www.ncte.org/books/tiow

9

Conducting Programmatic Assessment

- Support regular opportunities for program assessment.
- Promote end-of-year program reflection and revision.
- Survey and improve institutional resources and professional development.

Benchmarks, goals, and even curricular changes are easily pushed to back burners when the school year gets underway. It is easy to turn attention to disciplinary issues, testing requirements, or any number of other immediate concerns. Teachers will also be focused on multiple, everyday demands. Professional development, in addition to regular grade-level and content-area meetings, will help ensure that the writing initiative remains a priority. However, another essential tool is regular program assessment. Program assessment is not a punitive process; it is an important tool for helping teachers, departments, and school leaders see how much they have accomplished and to sharpen their focus on what still needs to be achieved. Programmatic assessment also provides opportunities for faculty / staff to reflect on the effectiveness of initiative-specific professional development and institutional supports. Together, this feedback will be invaluable as the school community continues to refine instruction and assessment, focus on best practices, and support the writing initiative.

Step 1: Support Regular Ongoing Opportunities for Program Assessment

Regular opportunities for program assessment will not only keep your school community focused on writing achievement, but they will also make end-of-year program assessments far more manageable and effective. It is recommended that you make one or more of these regular assessment strategies a monthly priority at grade-level and content-area meetings.

Curriculum Check-In

Curricula are excellent guides for teachers, but they shift and change with use. Units may take longer than teachers expect; students may struggle in unexpected areas and excel in others. Ask teachers to revisit their curricula regularly to reflect on what has worked, what needs improvement, what new areas of focus have emerged, and which areas have gone unaddressed. For instance, how are teachers incorporating best practices in content-area instruction (Chapter 4) into their curricula, and has this incorporation been effective? A science teacher may find that her curriculum supports students' writing in multiple, real-world genres, but that students have limited writing-to-learn opportunities. If this is the case, the teacher can think about ways to tweak her curriculum to offer more of these kinds of writing activities. Ask content-area and grade-level teams to fill out curriculum check-in checklists like this one and keep a running record of their reflections for use in future curriculum adjustments.

Curriculum Check-In

1. Which elements of this unit were most beneficial for student learning?
2. What specific writing skills did this unit promote?
3. Were all students successful at mastering these writing skills? Why or why not?
4. Which best practices in content-area instruction did this unit promote (writing-to-learn activities, the writing process, writing in multiple genres, the reading-writing connection)?

Benchmark Check-In

The school community should also reflect on departmental, grade-level, and schoolwide benchmarks. This can be accomplished in staff meetings, professional development sessions, or content-area and grade-level team meetings. Ask faculty/staff to examine the benchmarks they hoped to accomplish in a particular month. As with the curriculum check-in, ask departments to keep each month's check-in sheet as a record. Try to be supportive as they reflect on which benchmarks they have and have not met and what support they may require in meeting these and future benchmarks. This can also be an important opportunity for instructional leaders to determine whether a particular department, grade level, or teacher seems to be experiencing unique struggles. Strategizing with struggling faculty/staff to see what help they need, rather than taking a punitive stance, will work best. For example, if teachers

Benchmark Check-In

1. What benchmarks did you plan to meet this month?
2. Which benchmarks did you actually meet this month?
3. What allowed you to meet the benchmarks that you did?
4. What kept you from meeting other benchmarks?
5. What plan do you have for meeting these missed benchmarks in future months?
6. Are your benchmarks proving to be too ambitious? Not ambitious enough?
7. Do any important writing skills appear to be missing from your current benchmarks?

are struggling to work together as a grade-level team, you might offer to help facilitate their weekly meetings. Or if a new teacher is struggling with classroom management, you might arrange for a week of team-teaching in his or her classroom, so he or she can see a model of strong classroom management skills.

Instructional leaders can also model reflective pedagogical practices by being accountable to benchmarks themselves. Reflect monthly on the institutional benchmarks that your faculty/staff recommended. Which ones have been most successful? Which ones have not been accomplished on time? How will you resolve this? Talk openly with your faculty/staff about your reflections to show that this is a safe process. It can be tempting to make excuses to show that you're on top of your game; however, you'll never encourage faculty/staff to speak openly about their successes and areas for improvement if you don't do the same.

NCTE 9.1 *offers online versions of curriculum and benchmark check-ins.*

www.ncte.org/books/tiow

Step 2: End-of-Year Programmatic Assessment

Taking time at the end of the year to assess how the initiative is progressing is another crucial step for staying on track, inspiring faculty and staff, and communicating with your stakeholders. If you've been compiling curriculum and benchmark check-ins, the end-of-year assessment should go especially smoothly.

Compile Curriculum and Benchmark Check-Ins

With your writing initiative leadership teams, look over the check-ins your faculty/staff have completed. Begin looking for patterns. Have most benchmarks been met? Have certain writing skills been incorporated into the curriculum across the departments? What does your faculty/staff seem to be struggling with? What are they doing well? Take time in a staff meeting, professional development setting, or one-on-one to acknowledge everything your faculty/staff has accomplished, and come up with a plan for supporting faculty/staff, departments, or grade-level teams that seem to be struggling. This support may take the form of summer workshops, staffing decisions, or even schedule changes. Before making any drastic changes, however, get some feedback from faculty/staff about what might help them the most.

Assess Progress toward Meeting Schoolwide Writing Goals

While your benchmarks should help ensure that you are on your way to meeting your schoolwide writing goals, it is important to revisit them occasionally—in part, because they may have changed. As your faculty/staff learn more about good writing instruction, they may have new insights into what their students really need. They may learn that their writing goals were not ambitious enough or didn't take into account the real struggles their students would have with a certain writing goal. In combination with your conversation on benchmarks or standardized tests, or in a staff meeting of its own, create time for faculty and staff to revisit the schoolwide goals they created. You'll want to make sure that the meeting is structured in a way that allows every faculty/staff member's voice to be heard; this may mean working in small groups first or having individuals fill out a reflection sheet before a whole-group conversation. You may also want to compile some information ahead of time to make the conversation less loaded. For example, it could be helpful to report on how close you believe the school is to meeting each of its writing goals.

Communicating Progress to Stakeholders

1. Create a poster in the office, staff room, or school hallway that charts each benchmark you meet.

2. Send regular reports on benchmark and goal accomplishments to parents in a newsletter or post on your website.

3. Write personalized notes or emails to faculty and staff who have done an exceptional job of meeting school goals.

4. Revise report cards or add a supplement that acknowledges the strides each student is making in his or her writing.

5. Hold public events such as publishing parties, poetry readings, or science fairs and invite stakeholders to come see all the progress that has been made.

You might consider asking the following questions:

• Which writing goals are feeling the most manageable? Why?

• Which writing goals may be difficult to meet? Why?

• What support do you require to help you meet difficult writing goals?

• Should any writing goals be revised?

• Should any new writing goals be added?

Step 3: Survey and Revise Institutional Support and Professional Development

As you know, a successful writing initiative has solid institutional support. While you will have worked hard to predict which institutional supports and professional development will be most beneficial to the success of the writing initiative, you'll have many new ideas once the initiative is under way. Your faculty and staff will have many new ideas, too, so it's important to check in with them periodically.

Institutional Support

At the end of the year, it will be important to survey the faculty/staff to determine which institutional supports are the most effective in their teaching of writing and what supports they might still require. This will be most useful if you can compile a list of the institutional changes that have been put in place. The following categories might be the most useful to consider:

- Technology
- Schedule changes
- Support staff
- Assessment
- Class size
- Community involvement
- Grade-level and content-area teams
- Classroom space

Once you've received feedback from your faculty and staff, make a concerted effort to acknowledge all of it. Be realistic about which additional institutional supports are possible and get some feedback about the best way to proceed. Try not to be defensive about institutional supports that faculty and staff haven't found to be effective; instead, ask for feedback about how they might be improved and do your best to make concrete and visible changes.

Institutional Support Survey

1. Which institutional changes have most benefited your students' writing achievement? In what ways?
2. Have any institutional changes detracted from your students' learning? How?
3. What further institutional changes would most benefit your students' ability to meet schoolwide writing goals? Content-area and grade-level benchmarks?

Professional Development

By providing faculty/staff with regular opportunities to provide feedback on professional development sessions, you accomplish at least three things: (1) you encourage teachers to reflect on their own professional growth; (2) you provide a productive forum for faculty/staff to voice opinions and concerns about the nature of their training; (3) you can help ensure that future PD sessions are even more beneficial to your faculty's/staff's development.

Consider handing out a short survey after each professional development session. In addition to the survey, you might check in informally with faculty/staff who seemed especially engaged, concerned, inquisitive, or confused in the session. You can learn a lot in a three-minute conversation in the hallway. However you decide to proceed, make sure you respond to the surveys. A simple acknowledgment at the beginning of the next PD session that you appreciated faculty/staff responses will go a long way; they might also appreciate hearing what you plan to do with their feedback. If the session with your consultant went well, say that you're planning to invite them back. If an e-portfolio training session was too rudimentary for some and too challenging for others, explain that you'll split into two self-selecting groups for the next technology session.

End-of-year assessments of professional development are also an important opportunity for faculty/staff to make their voices heard and for school leaders to reflect more holistically on what sorts of staff development have worked well and what needs to be improved. Consider a longer survey for collecting this feedback. As with regular professional development feedback, it is important that school leaders be as transparent as possible when responding to this feedback. Ask yourself: What information was helpful to receive? What professional development gaps or concerns have you identified? What plans do you have to improve professional development?

End-of-Year PD Survey

1. Which PD sessions most improved your teaching of writing?
2. What about these sessions worked?
3. Which PD sessions were not especially helpful?
4. What about these sessions made them helpful?
5. Do you have any suggestions for how to improve professional development sessions?
6. Are there any professional development topics you would especially like to see included in next year's schedule?

Sample Professional Development Survey
Topic: Responding to student writing
The facilitator was knowledgeable.
   1   2   3   4   5
I learned important new strategies for responding to student writing in this session.
   1   2   3   4   5
I plan to use these strategies in my classroom.
   1   2   3   4   5
The strategies suggested today correspond to my own teaching philosophy.
   1   2   3   4   5
I would like more PD sessions on this topic.
   1   2   3   4   5

Step 4: Affirm and Support Stakeholders

As an instructional leader, you know that the success of any initiative depends on the contributions of those who are most deeply committed to it. The evaluation phase of the writing initiative is a good time to acknowledge these contributions. No doubt you can think of many ways to affirm the work of those who are contributing most to the initiative, but we include a few suggestions here:

- Send personal messages of appreciation.
- Contact local media outlets to do a feature that focuses on key contributors to the writing initiative.
- Nominate key stakeholders for local and/or national awards.
- Invite students to write tributes to teachers, community members, and members of the staff who have provided helpful instruction.
- Invite a panel of graduates to talk about how the writing initiative has helped them in college or the workplace.
- Mount a celebration of student writing.
- Seek support of your school's parent association to sponsor an appreciation event such as a breakfast before school or an after-school reception.

Support for Stakeholders

This can be even more important than expressions of appreciation or affirmation. Those who care deeply about the writing initiative will probably be most grateful for your efforts to support *their* efforts. To do this effectively, you may need to gather information from stakeholders themselves. This can also be an opportunity to be sure that you have an accurate list of those who made the most significant contributions to the project. Questions such as the following can be asked directly or incorporated into a survey:

1. What made your work with the writing initiative go smoothly?
2. What were the difficulties you encountered in working with the writing initiative?
3. In your view, what would have made the writing initiative more effective?
4. If you could have just one thing to improve the writing initiative, what would it be?
5. List the individuals who were most helpful to you in carrying out your part of the writing initiative.

NCTE 9.2 *offers online versions of surveys for steps 3 and 4.*

www.ncte.org/books/tiow

Step 5: Generate Reports on the Overall Effects of the Initiative

Given your many responsibilities, it is probably not realistic for you to write lengthy reports about the writing initiative at your school, but there are a number of ways to make the initiative more visible, and many of these can be completed by others. Here are some suggestions:

- Repurpose the evaluative data to create a quantitative summary of the project.
- Recruit student journalists to write a feature on the writing initiative from the student perspective.
- Ask the art instructor or another faculty member with good graphic skills to make a timeline display of the steps of the writing initiative.
- Ask selected teachers to create a display of student writing.
- Invite selected students to make a presentation to the school board about their experience in the writing initiative.
- Ask teachers in subjects other than English to explain—either in a recording or in writing—how the writing initiative changed their teaching.
- Invite representatives of the local media to visit your school for presentations on the writing initiative from teachers and students.

By reaching out to multiple audiences, including faculty and students in your school, these reports can contribute to the vitality of the writing initiative because those who make the reports can be reinvigorated by reviewing their own participation.

As you probably know, one of the chief problems with many educational reforms is that they are not sustained. Too often an initiative is undertaken one year and abandoned a year or two later, leaving stakeholders feeling somewhat betrayed and uncertain about whether to invest themselves in the next initiative. For students to receive the full benefit of a writing initiative, you need to focus on it for several years. The process of evaluating the project and reviewing action steps can help you develop plans for sustaining the writing initiative so that it continues for more than a year or two. Among the factors that help to sustain educational initiatives are building innovation into daily routines, establishing collaborative practices focused on instructional goals, adaptation of structures to support the innovation, consistency in school and district goals, and awareness of the political context.

Incorporate innovation into daily routines.
This makes it much more likely that an initiative will be sustained. In the case of the writing initiative, it is especially true that teachers who become accustomed to incorporating writing into their teaching will continue doing it, especially if they see the benefits of using writing as a way of learning.

Continue programmatic assessment.
The establishment of guidelines developed in Chapter 2 can provide an indicator to measure the extent to which content-area and/or grade-level groups are meeting the goals and benchmarks they established for themselves.

Establishing collaborative practices focused on instructional goals.
This means that everyone in the school works together toward a common end, and the steps outlined in this book should help faculty and staff to support a shared commitment to the writing initiative. The key issue will be to ensure that newcomers are incorporated into the collaboration. This will require *ongoing professional development for new hires* in the school. Such attention to turnover in personnel will ensure that the collaborative spirit established by the writing initiative will be sustained.

Adapt school structures to support an innovation.
This is another strategy for ensuring sustainability. As the steps outlined in Chapter 7 explain, there are many ways to adapt school structures to support the writing initiative, and maintaining those structural changes will help to sustain the writing initiative.

Maintaining awareness of the political context.
At the most local level, this means attending to the community in which the school is located, and at the other end of the spectrum, it means discerning how national policy initiatives will shape instruction more generally. The processes of recruiting community stakeholders for the writing initiative, maintaining communication with them throughout the process, and sharing with them reports

of results such as those described in this chapter will address the local political scene. The current attention to Common Core Standards for English language arts has the potential to shape writing instruction, and it will be important to monitor how your state interprets and responds to this initiative. In any event, you can be assured that a writing initiative will be well received in the current political climate.

Implementation Scenario: Making Successes Visible

A high school in Minnesota focused its writing initiative on improving student writing in the content areas. Teachers in all disciplines required students to keep a writer's notebook in which they wrote reflections on and questions about what they were studying; they also made a habit of asking students to write brief summaries of what they had learned at the end of class; and they showed students how the schoolwide rubric applied to their classes, using it to evaluate written assignments.

When many students' scores improved by two points on the state test, the principal sent an email blast and tweet to all stakeholders, including the student body, teachers, parents, school board, and community members. She also posted the good news on their school website's homepage, using the headline "Students Demonstrate Growth as Writers." In the posting, she complimented teachers and students for their efforts and reiterated their goal to persist in improving student writing.

> **NCTE 9.3** *offers more examples of instructional leaders implementing principles from this chapter.*
>
> www.ncte.org/books/tiow

Appendix

Apply for NCTE Certification of Excellence for Writing Initiative

In recognition of the importance of enhancing writing instruction, NCTE has established a process by which instructional leaders can receive recognition for creating effective writing initiatives.

> **NCTE 10.1** *provides the application form for Certification of Excellence for Writing Initiative.*
>
> www.ncte.org/books/tiow

About the Authors

Anne Ruggles Gere is Gertrude Buck Collegiate Professor at the University of Michigan where she directs the Sweetland Center for Writing and the Joint PhD Program in English and Education. A former president of NCTE and currently the director of NCTE's Squire Office of Policy Research, she has published a dozen books and more than seventy articles, many of them about the teaching of writing.

Hannah A. Dickinson is a doctoral candidate in the Joint PhD Program in English and Education. Her dissertation focuses on students' academic writing about violence and how teachers can and do respond to such writing. While at Michigan, Hannah has mentored new college writing instructors, worked as a consultant for Michigan's Center on Teaching and Learning, and helped design a program to improve college access for high school students in Detroit. Before entering graduate school, she taught humanities at a public middle school in New York City.

Melinda J. McBee Orzulak is a doctoral candidate at the University of Michigan in the Joint PhD Program in English and Education. Her research focuses on how to better support beginning English teachers in enacting linguistically informed principles that support equitable learning. Before graduate school, she taught high school humanities and supervised English, writing, world language, and social science teachers in Chicago. She also taught in Boston as part of the Tufts University Urban Teacher Training Collaborative and at alternative schools in Kansas City.

Stephanie Moody is a PhD candidate in the Joint PhD Program in English and Education at the University of Michigan. Before moving to Michigan, Stephanie taught high school English in Illinois for five years. Her research interests include literacy and gender, students' out-of-class literacy practices, and the teaching of composition.

This book was typeset in TheMix and Palatino by Barbara Frazier.

The typeface used on the cover is Frutiger Light.

The book was printed on 50-lb. Williamsburg Offset paper by Versa Press, Inc.